W9-BYV-541

MAINTENANCE AND REPAIR
OF WIND
AND PERCUSSION
INSTRUMENTS

Maintenance and Repair of Wind and Percussion Instruments

George H. Springer

A HANDBOOK FOR DIRECTORS AND INSTRUMENTALISTS

ALLYN AND BACON, INC.
Boston • London • Sydney

788.052
Sp83m

C. C. HARDY LIBRARY
ATLANTIC CHRISTIAN COLLEGE
WILSON, N. C. 27893

Copyright © 1976 by Allyn and Bacon, Inc., 470 Atlantic Avenue, Boston, Massachusetts 02210.

All rights reserved. Printed in the United States of America. No part of the material protected by this copyright notice may be reproduced or utilized in any form or by any means, electronic or mechanical, including photocopying, recording, or by any information storage and retrieval system, without written permission from the copyright owner.

Portions of this book first appeared in *Maintenance and Repair of Band Instruments: For Band Directors and Instrumentalists* by George H. Springer. Copyright © 1970 by Allyn and Bacon, Inc.

Library of Congress Cataloging in Publication Data

Springer, George H
  Maintenance and repair of wind and percussion instruments.

  1970 ed. published under title: Maintenance and repair of band instruments.
  Bibliography: p.
  Includes index.
  1. Wind instruments—Repairing. 2. Percussion instruments—Repairing. I. Title.
ML930.S74 1976   788′.05′2   75-31663
ISBN 0-205-05012-3

Acknowledgements

I extend my sincere appreciation to: B. A. Nugent, Albert Fitzgerrel, David Salsbury, Theresa Turley, Esther Stegemann, James Fleisher, and Edmund C. Williams.

NOV 11 1976

76— 1278

Contents

3 Suggested Repair Equipment   45

4 Standard Repairs   53

5 Most Frequent Problems   127

Preface

As a band director I have seen the satisfying results of a systematic program of care, maintenance, and repair. In every band there have been students who were eager and capable of performing maintenance and repair problems that, normally, would have been sent to a repair shop, robbed the director of valuable time needed for other matters, or interrupted a rehearsal.

As a clinician I have discovered that few directors have the needed background in care, maintenance, and repair, but most are eager to learn. Also, many valuable suggestions have come from directors attending these clinics. Those suggestions have been added to this edition.

As a repairman I have seen the justification for this manual. A large percentage of repairs could be avoided by conscientious care and maintenance practices.

George H. Springer
Montalba, Texas

Introduction

One of the side benefits of attending a music convention is the discovery that all band directors have similar problems. When large assemblies are dismissed and dissolve into the small intimate groups that invariably dot the convention center lobby, the conversation often turns to the ludicrous accidents that occasionally befall each director. If one of the stories concerns the twisting of a neckpipe, the breaking of braces, or the warping of tuning slides, most of the experienced directors in the circle will nod with understanding.

Repairmen, too, have their stories and share mutual experiences. One story that is often told concerns a customer who drove over 100 miles to get an expensive saxophone repaired for a forthcoming program, only to discover that the inoperative G$\sharp$ key was caused by an unhooked spring.

Although every band director cannot be a proficient repairman, learning a few basic facts and techniques wil save many lost student-hours and frustrations. When *all* students play instruments that are kept in good condition, every aspect of musicianship will improve.

Many repairmen are ex-directors or professional musicians who often understand the director's problems better than the director understands the repair business. A repairman's income is usually determined by the amount of *time* he spends in repairing. Show respect for his time, and you will probably never need to complain about his service.

If, on the other hand, the repairman fails consistently to meet the promised date for repairs and is careless in his work, he is not showing respect for the customer's obligations and should not be considered for future business.

A review of repair manuals, care and maintenance pamphlets, and repair chapters in music education textbooks reveals one of the reasons why band directors and instrumentalists are often weak in this phase of their profession. Following are some of the findings in repair literature:

1. Some repair practices presented to the novice as standard procedures are of a questionable nature.

2. Sometimes identical or similar illustrations and procedures are given for several instrument repairs when one presentation would suffice.

3. A maze of details and illustrations, unnecessary even for the novice—and sometimes confusing—often accompanies simple procedures outlined adequately in the text.

4. The "knack" of using makeshift equipment is, seemingly, given more emphasis than proper repair procedures.

5. Some texts refer simple problems to the repair shop. With no instructions available, instrumentalists in remote areas must "experiment" or lose valuable time by shipping instruments to a repairman.

6. Accurate information prepared by expert repairmen is often too general, too limited in scope, or too advanced for many directors and instrumentalists to comprehend.

An attempt has been made in this book to eliminate duplication by first presenting procedures that are common to several instruments, followed by instructions pertaining to specific instruments. The solution to each repair problem is given in a step-by-step approach that is intended to be brief and to the point.

In addition to the Contents and the Index, the text is organized to aid the reader in locating a subject by heading. Following the chapter heading is the first large division, such as Brass, followed by a smaller subdivision, such as French Horn, and a side heading for specific problems—for example, Repairing Stuck Valves. Many illustrations are given to clarify the instructions. Asterisks follow words that are identified in the "Terminology" chapter.

This book is based upon the writer's personal experiences during thirteen years as a band director in the public schools (grades 4 through 12), and on experience gained in more than six years as the owner of a repair shop in Dallas and Montalba, Texas, where he served both amateur and professional musicians.

Care and Maintenance 1

Thousands of dollars are spent each year by instrument manufacturers on free literature to aid the band director in discharging his duties. But this literature can be of no benefit unless properly used. Included in such publications are care and maintenance pamphlets that can assist in the elimination of many annoying repair problems.

Though the frequency of presentation will vary according to the method used, proper care of instruments should be taught as faithfully as any other aspect of music instruction.

Instrument inspection is often one of the requirements in marching contests and the director must conform to whatever military style procedures are customary in his region. It is doubtful, however, if a "by the numbers" inspection, even though impressive, can be as effective as an examination by a conscientious director who is thoroughly familiar with good care and maintenance practices.

Although many directors have eliminated the following problems, others may discover tips that will help them in their prevention.

GENERAL PRECAUTIONS

Damage to instruments is most frequently caused by inexperienced handling.
Unless it is part of a definite teaching program, students should not play each
other's instruments!

Cases should be kept as near as possible to performance areas. All instruments should be placed in cases when not in the students' own hands. Even if
attendants are present in a partitioned band section of the bleachers during the
third-quarter break, seat vibrations from an adjoining section of the bleachers or
an excited youngster racing through the band section can cause damage to uncased instruments. Having the case nearby also helps if a sudden rainstorm should
occur.

Thoughtful planning is needed in storing instruments such as the sousaphone, or percussion and mallet instruments. The urge to "bang" on the percussion instruments or throw trash in the sousaphones is a normal tendency of
human behavior. A shortage of storage space need be no problem. A hinged,
four-sided box of 1/8-inch fibreboard can be easily constructed to cover the timpani, marimba, and other such instruments not being used. Sousaphones and
glockenspiels can be suspended from wall hooks just above the players' chairs, and
sousaphone bell covers can be made of cheesecloth with an elastic edge for easy
removal. Most teachers of art and home economics will assist in the design and
construction of attractive covers that can be used at half-time shows and parades
as well as serving as a deterrent for trash accumulation.

Poorly designed instrument lockers that necessitate stacking, crowding, or
storing in unconventional positions; lockers located near exits or in congested
hallways; and storage rooms with only one door contribute to instrument damage.
If such conditions exist and cannot be remedied, rehearsals should be ended a few
minutes early in order to prevent the frantic last-minute rush for lockers. An early
dismissal also allows time for proper woodwind swabbing.

The band trip is another cause of instrument damage. Warped trombone
slides, dented sousaphones, and broken drumheads frequently result from hasty
loadings. Packing quilts can be purchased for a fraction of the cost of bass drumheads and major repair work on sousaphones. Careful loading by a dependable
band manager can prevent damage to all of the instruments.

Eating candy, chewing gum, and drinking carbonated beverages just before
(or while) playing can cause dirty mouthpieces, sticking pads, sluggish valves, corroded slides, and poor intonation. This often occurs during the third-quarter
break. Though the director cannot deny his students a period of relaxation, he
can and should develop some practical means of alleviating this problem. A highly
successful director at one school has all wind players rinse their mouths with
water before returning to their seats after the third-quarter break.

IMPORTANCE OF THE INSTRUMENT CASE

The importance of a good instrument case has been overlooked by nearly everyone except the zealous musician and manufacturer. From the days when the cardboard case, the **drawstring sack***, the **doc's bag,** or the **smuggler's case** could be purchased for a few dollars comes the mistaken notion that a new trumpet case costing fifteen percent as much as a student trumpet is the best type of case to buy. Despite its sturdy appearance, it is usually constructed of specially treated cardboard no thicker than a hardback book cover. However, such a case may be adequate if the instrument fits into it properly, the straps or **turnbuttons** adjust snugly, and the case latches function correctly. Too often when a student fails to fasten the instrument after placing it in the case, the lid will unexpectedly open (due to a faulty latch) and the instrument will fall out. A dollar's worth of materials and a few minutes of time can often prevent such mishaps.

A student who refuses to have a faulty case latch replaced by the luggage shop repairman because it does not match the old one—or the student who intends to wait until he can find just the right shade of velvet before he replaces the broken turnbutton—is only inviting trouble.

Loose articles (valve oil, lyres, mouthpieces, key oil, cork grease, screwdrivers, pliers, case deodorizers, reed clippers, swabs, atomizers, ligatures, mouthpiece caps, etc.) inside the case will eventually cause damage. Small, unsightly dents in brass instruments, including the valve **casings**, are the result of failure to place accessories in the accessory compartment. Bent keys, chipped tone holes, and torn pad skins are casualties that plague the careless woodwind player. The saxophonist who is indifferent to loose articles will ultimately find that the "stuffy" sound his instrument has suddenly acquired is caused by a ligature or mouthpiece cap that has become lodged inside the upper body. If a case does not have an accessory compartment, a homemade drawstring sack will be sufficient.

The woodwind player who allows rubber bands, bits and pieces of cork, chamois, sponge rubber, chewing gum wrappers, old reeds, and lunch money to accumulate inside the case is sure to visit the repair shop needlessly. Stopped up **tone holes** and inoperative keys are the most frequent consequences of an untidy case.

Gym shorts, tennis shoes, folding music racks, bulky method books, and sack lunches, crowded into the case, are other causes of instrument damage. No case, however strong, can prevent impairment of the instrument if this practice is followed.

*Terms in bold type are defined in the Terminology section in the back of the book.

Although aesthetically poor, a case handle made of baling wire or a wire coat hanger covered with tape is safer than a weakly constructed or worn-out handle. Damage can occur when a cased instrument is dropped from only waist height. The bicycle-riding bandsman who slips the case handle over the handlebars is following a dangerous practice. Much more serious than the damage to the instrument is the possibility of bodily injuries caused from hard bumps or sudden turns, since the instrument can become wedged between the front wheel and frame and send the student sprawling.

Even after every precaution has been taken by the director and students, the instrument will sometimes be involved in unavoidable accidents. The best insurance against damage is a sturdy case that is properly fitted to the instrument and *securely fastened inside.*

WOODWINDS

Swabbing

One of the most important items of woodwind care is the routine of *careful* swabbing after playing. Though there is disagreement among musicians as to whether moisture causes wooden instruments to crack, keeping instruments free of moisture will not only eliminate that possibility but will prevent a build-up of grime inside the bore—a major factor in intonation problems.

The turkey feather has been the traditional oboe swab for many years, but it is becoming less frequently used due to lack of availability and the development of commercial swabs that will dry more thoroughly. One such swab is a soft, vinyl-covered cable with a small sponge that can be drawn completely through the upper joint.

Bassoon, clarinet, flute, piccolo, and saxophone swabs (Figure 112, page 189) are available for drying all parts of the instruments and *should be used diligently.*

Bore Oiling

There is also controversy over the necessity for oiling the bores of wooden instruments, but a careful, periodic oiling will do no harm and might possibly prevent cracking. The following steps should be observed:

1. Allow at least one day's drying time before oiling.

2. Select a good bore oil, olive oil, or almond oil.

3. Use a clean cloth or chamois swab with a few drops of oil and draw it through the bore several times. To prevent excessive oil from soaking pads, insert a piece of wax paper under each of the closed key pads.

4. Let the instrument dry overnight if possible.

Here again, opinions vary widely on the frequency of oiling. Some believe that a new instrument should be oiled twice a week, while others feel that once a month is sufficient. The safest course to follow is the one recommended by the manufacturer or dealer to whom the instrument will be sent for adjustment if it should crack within the warranty period. The following schedule for oiling will be acceptable to most users: once a week for the first two months, once a month for the next ten months, and every six months thereafter. Whatever oiling frequency a director may choose for his teaching of care and maintenance, it is imperative that he be consistent if he expects the students to follow his instructions.

Since the upper joints on most bassoons are treated with moisture-resisting agents and the boot joint is rubber- (or metal-) lined, the bores should not be oiled unless so specified by the manufacturer.

Temperature and Humidity

Most pamphlets on woodwind care contain a warning against temperature extremes, but the repairman must still occasionally **pin** or **band** a wooden instrument that had been placed in a refrigerator or oven by a student who was trying to shrink a stuck **tenon.** Cold instruments should be warmed gradually at room temperature before playing. Setting the instrument near a fireplace, radiator, or furnace vent is not advisable! Sudden changes of humidity should also be avoided if possible.

Key Oiling

A thorough oiling of metal hinge and pivot points and saxophone **key rollers** once a month will assure smooth operation of keys and prevent formation of rust from perspiration acids. A key oil with a thin wire attached to the bottle cap is the most convenient to use, since it releases only a small drop of oil wherever its tip is placed. In the absence of that type of applicator, a round toothpick, needle, or small wire may be used by dipping it into the oil. Care must be taken to prevent excessive oil from collecting around **posts** and from saturating the pads. Pipe cleaners can be used for absorbing excessive oil around the posts and in places difficult to reach with a cloth. A small artist's brush is a good accessory for removing the accumulation of dust around keys and posts.

Tone Holes

The accumulation of dirt and grime in the tone holes of oboes and clarinets is especially common. As the application of only one thin coat of **tuning oil** on a given tone hole will alter its pitch (a common repair practice for tuning wooden instruments), several tone holes coated with *dirt* or *grime* makes proper intonation impossible. By using a pipe cleaner or cotton swab, the player can keep the tone holes clean with very little effort.

Tenons

Dryness is the most common cause of loose or frayed **tenon** corks. Cork grease can be purchased at almost any music store or repair shop and should be used periodically to keep the cork "live," and to allow ease in assembling. **Mutton tallow** may be used as a satisfactory substitute for cork grease.

Broken tenons and warped keys are often the results of the pressure caused by the necessity of gripping the woodwind joint too tightly while assembling. If excessive pressure is caused by a moisture-saturated, swelled tenon rather than a dry cork, consult the "Standard Repairs" chapter for procedures.

Improper care is another cause of chipped, worn, or broken tenons. The middle tenons on the clarinet and oboe, the foot tenon on the flute, and the tenor joint on the bassoon are points of unavoidable, structural weakness. Dropping or bumping assembled instruments will often cause expensive or irreparable damage. Laying an assembled woodwind instrument on a bed or chair is inviting disaster. Unsuspecting persons may accidentally sit on instruments that have been carelessly covered by an article of clothing, a sheet, or a bedspread. Carelessness by a band member in passing through a door with an improperly operating closer may cause instrument damage, if the door should slam shut against the assembled instrument.

Though some instrument manufacturers do not provide **tenon caps** for new instruments, caps may be purchased separately from music stores or repair shops. Not only does the tenon cap offer protection from breaking or chipping, it prevents accumulation of dust and trash on the greased tenon and discoloration of the case lining (Figure 109, page 188).

Particularly desirable are oboe tenon caps with felt washers that have been saturated with almond oil to prevent cracking. Players who have used them attest to their effectiveness.

The tenon that has become worn through long usage and allows leakage or looseness (despite the application of a new, thicker tenon cork) should be sent to the repair shop for installation of tenon caps (or shims).

Octave Tube

The **octave tube**, inserted through the body of most woodwinds at the octave (or register) key, extends into the **bore** to prevent water from entering the hole. This tube may become clogged occasionally by a particle from the swab. A broom straw or small, stiff bristle may be used to free the obstruction without removing the key. This opening is exceptionally critical, especially on the bassoon **nib**, and should not be cleaned with hard metal objects that will enlarge the hole. Accumulated water may be removed from octave tubes on smaller instruments by blowing air through the upper joint while closing all openings except the octave or register key. A common desk blotter can be a valuable asset for instruments that are prone to accumulate excessive amounts of water.

For more serious problems involving the octave tube, consult the "Standard Repairs" chapter.

Mouthpiece

Three out of four clarinet and saxophone mouthpieces must be acid cleaned to remove the accumulated deposits caused by improper cleaning. The resonating **chamber** of a woodwind mouthpiece is as sensitive as the resonating chamber on a fine violin and should be kept free of obstructions.

When played daily, clarinet and saxophone mouthpieces should be cleaned at least *once a week;* otherwise, saliva acids will cause chalky deposits that cannot be removed with soap and water. Some band directors have enlisted the aid of the science teacher in solving the problem of keeping mouthpieces clean. A sample of the deposits in a dirty mouthpiece, when placed on a slide under a microscope with an overhead projector, will change the sanitation habits of the most careless player.

A mouthpiece brush may be used, but care must be exercised when applying the brush to avoid scratching the mouthpiece parts. It is safer to use a soft cloth with *lukewarm* water and bland soap. Since both plastic and hard rubber mouthpieces are susceptible to heat warpage, they *should not be cleaned in hot water!*

Mouthpieces of good quality can be restored to useable condition, even though they have been warped or contain deposits that cannot be removed with bland soap. These problems are covered in the "Standard Repairs" chapter.

Saxophone End Plugs

Like the tenon cap, the **end plug** is essential for protecting the instrument while it is in the case. A major cause of damage to the alto and tenor saxophone octave mechanisms is the failure of the player to insert the end plug before placing the saxophone in the case (Figure 103, page 142). The **octave bridge** on most alto and tenor saxophones extends beyond the **tenon receiver** and is made of soft brass. The slightest bump will often throw the automatic octave mechanism out of adjustment if the instrument has been placed in the case without an end plug.

Saxophone octave problems that cannot be corrected by the band director should be brought to the attention of an experienced repairman.

Saxophone Drying

The saxophone is, without question, the most poorly cared for instrument in the woodwind family. Unsanitary deposits are found in a majority of saxophones from the **neckpipe** to the **bell bow**. Saliva accumulations are responsible for dried out (and leaking) pads, poor intonation, and for pads whose skins have been eaten away by acids.

The construction of saxophones varies somewhat, but the pads that collect moisture on most saxophones are the low $D^\sharp$ ($E^\flat$), the **palm keys**, and the $G^\sharp$. Thorough swabbing will alleviate the pad soaking that normally results if a saxophone is put in the case "wet." The application of neatsfoot oil to the affected pads will eliminate saturation of the pads while in playing position. It also keeps the pads supple, and it will assure longer service.

Cleaning the Neckpipe and Bocal

If the director has been negligent in maintaining proper instrument care, he will find that the saxophone neckpipes and bassoon **bocals** contain accumulated grime and require special cleaning. After removing the octave key on the saxophone neckpipe, place it and the bocal in lukewarm, soapy water. Let them soak. A flexible brush (available at music stores) may be used for further cleaning of the saxophone neckpipe (Figure 112, page 189). Special brushes are now available for cleaning bocals and may be purchased from professional bassoonists and from some music stores. In the absence of a bocal brush, long, joined sections of pipe cleaners and numerous flushings will be necessary to remove accumulations.

Since the bassoon bocal cannot be swabbed effectively after each playing, a weekly washing is necessary to keep its bore free of dirt. Swabbing the saxophone neckpipe after each playing will eliminate the need for a periodic scrubbing.

Protecting the Finish

Acids from the human body are damaging to an instrument, even though it may have the "epoxy" type lacquer, nickel-plated keys, or a body and keys made of nickel and silver alloys. Continued handling can eventually tarnish or wear any material, but the destructive action of body chemicals can be slowed significantly if the player will wipe fingerprints and saliva from the body and keys after each playing. A variety of wipe cloths, containing special chemicals for counteracting body acids on lacquer and silver instruments, is available from most music dealers. Conscientious use of these cloths will preserve the finish.

BRASSES

General Remarks

Despite the fact that "care and maintenance" instructions contain adequate cleaning tips for brass instruments, unnecessary and costly repairs are frequent in the repair business. A typical example is a "rotted" **mouthpipe.** The first indication of this problem is the appearance of small, pink spots under the lacquer. These spots will soon develop into irreparable leaks. A new factory mouthpipe that is properly installed, polished, and lacquered will range in cost from ten to twenty-five percent of the price of the instrument, depending on the brand and type. This is an expense that can be eliminated by proper care.

Piston Valve Instrument Cleaning

When a brass instrument is played daily, it should be thoroughly washed in warm, soapy water, with the valves removed and all slides pulled, *at least every two weeks.* During each washing, the mouthpipe should be cleaned with a flexible brush (Figure 112, page 189) to remove the deposits to which it is most susceptible. The flexible brush should also be used on tubings and around the valve **knuckles,** where a greenish corrosion often appears. The flexible brush should not be forced into the sharply curved bows of the small tuning slides, as it can become lodged inside the bow. Care must be observed when cleaning around the valve casings to prevent the scoring of valve walls and the formation of burrs, which will hinder valve action.

Pistons should be soaked carefully in a separate container to prevent dents and scratches from contact with other metal parts. The walls of **ports** are delicate and should be cleaned gingerly with a soft brush to remove the film that invariably forms there.

Trombone Cleaning

Flexible brushes are available for reaching the hand **slide bow** (Figure 112, page 189) and should be used at least every two weeks to prevent a buildup of deposits. After cleaning with a soapy solution, flush with clean water. Then use the rigid rod for cleaning and drying the slide walls. The rod should be completely covered with a cloth so that no metal part can touch the walls. Enough surplus cloth should be left extending over the handle so that it can be firmly grasped to prevent its becoming lodged inside the tubing.

Most manufacturers recommend that the inside slides be cleaned with a weighted cord and cloth similar to the type used in clarinet cleaning, since the inside walls are more delicate than the outer slide. Cleaning the insides of the inner slides will prevent a buildup of slime, which is prevalent in the trombone. The outer surface of the inner slides should be cleaned with a clean cloth dampened by a nonabrasive liquid, such as kerosene. The use of wood alcohol or lacquer thinner should be avoided, since a drop of these liquids will damage some lacquer finishes. Unless the **stockings** have troublesome deposits that cannot be removed by a nonabrasive compound, the director should not allow them to be buffed by a repairman. These stockings have been precision-fitted to allow easy slide operation with a minimum of leakage. Buffing by harsh abrasives will remove valuable plating and destroy the snug fit.

Only the slide being cleaned should be held while cleaning. Otherwise, a warped slide may result.

Often overlooked in trombone cleaning are the **cork barrels.** Dirt left inside the barrels will eventually work down to the slide surfaces and cause trouble. Feathers, pipe cleaners, small paint brushes, or water under pressure can be utilized for cleaning this area.

The tuning slide and the tubing on trombones with the F attachment may be cleaned with a flexible brush in the same manner as the piston valve instruments.

Rotary Valve Instruments

The mouthpipe of the French horn is more susceptible to acid damage than that of any other instrument and should be washed and swabbed *at least every two weeks.* Some horns have a tuning slide on the end of the mouthpipe, which will allow the flexible brush (Figure 112, page 189) to pass completely through, thereby pushing the deposits outside. On horns whose mouthpipe connects to tubing that leads to a valve, the valve must be removed (see Figure 81, page 113), the flexible rod inserted as far as possible, and the mouthpipe flushed with water under pressure.

If the mouthpipe is cleaned consistently, a thorough "bathtub" cleaning, with all slides pulled and all valves removed, will be necessary only two or three times a year. At such times, the **rotary valves**, the **stems**, and the **bearing washers** should be scrubbed and oiled. In cleaning the tubings, do not try to force the flexible brush all the way through any of the valve tuning slides or through any stationary tubing with radical curves. To prevent future trouble, the valves should be restrung with new cord (see Figure 78, page 111).

Between cleaning periods, a thorough flushing of rotary valves with kerosene, lighter fluid, or penetrating oil will remove the saliva residue that can build up around the bearing surfaces and prevent valve oil from reaching the critical points. Flushing is especially effective for new instruments whose bearing tolerances are extremely small.

Sousaphone and Tuba Cleaning

The sousaphone, like the French horn, cannot be cleaned as easily as the smaller, piston valve instruments. However, the director can see that the valves are removed and cleaned and that the mouthpipe, **tuning bits**, tuning slides, and **gooseneck** are scrubbed frequently. The necessity of diligence in such cleaning is evidenced by the filmy buildup in the valve ports, and the necessity for frequent replacement of the gooseneck and mouthpipe.

Unless the band director is fortunate enough to have school facilities that can accommodate tuba and sousaphone cleanings, it is more practical to have these instruments cleaned once a year in a repair shop.

Some directors have their tuba players use the garden hose for cleaning loose deposits and for flushing trash from sousaphones and tubas. This method will alleviate some problems, but it should not replace the methodical techniques previously mentioned.

Summer Cleaning

The lure of summer vacation affects the band director as much as it does his students, but the year's work is not complete until he is assured that all school brasses not going to the repair shop have been thoroughly cleaned *and dried* before storing. This should be done faithfully, whether the instruments are cleaned personally or by someone else.

Slide Greasing

After each washing, slides should be greased with cork grease or mutton tallow. Where possible, the grease should be applied to each **tube** separately, inserted into the **sleeve** of the tube, and worked back and forth in a spiralling motion to coat the entire surface.

The tuning slides that are operated while playing, such as the first and third slides on cornets and trumpets, and the main tuning slide on some tubas, should be lubricated with a lighter solution. Castor oil, mineral oil, or a mixture of either with valve oil are liquids used by some professionals to assure maximum sealing and smooth operation.

Valve Oiling

A variety of opinions has been expressed concerning the need for and the frequency of valve oiling, but a repairman who has witnessed the destructive action of saliva acids and the wearing effect on **pistons** from dry operation will attest to the necessity for oiling. One drop on each piston before playing will assure smooth operation and protect the finish against acids.

French horns that do not have hollow **stems** for oiling should be oiled by placing several drops into the appropriate slide. Turn the instrument so that the oil will reach both ends of the rotary valve and simultaneously operate the valve **levers**. To make sure that oil reaches the critical points, the **valve caps** should be removed and oil placed in the center of each bearing washer. Since many rotary valve problems are caused by dry or corroded stems on the bearing washer side, the necessity for keeping these parts oiled is obvious.

PERCUSSIONS

Storing

Vital budget money can be saved each year if the director will devote a little attention to the proper storage of the percussion instruments. Valuable storage and protective devices can be devised easily and with little expense. This will completely eliminate damage or loss. Figures 1, 2, and 3 illustrate only one of many solutions for storing mallets, sticks, and cymbals.

Brackets can be made from scrap material and mounted on a cabinet, a wall, or a door near the percussion section. A quick check by the percussion leader at the end of each band period will eliminate loss or misplacement.

In addition to the hinged, fibreboard protector (see "General Precautions," page 4), padded covers (available at music stores), or muslin covers, made by a local upholstery firm, seat cover shop, or home economics department, will offer protection against dust, fingerprints, and unauthorized tampering.

15

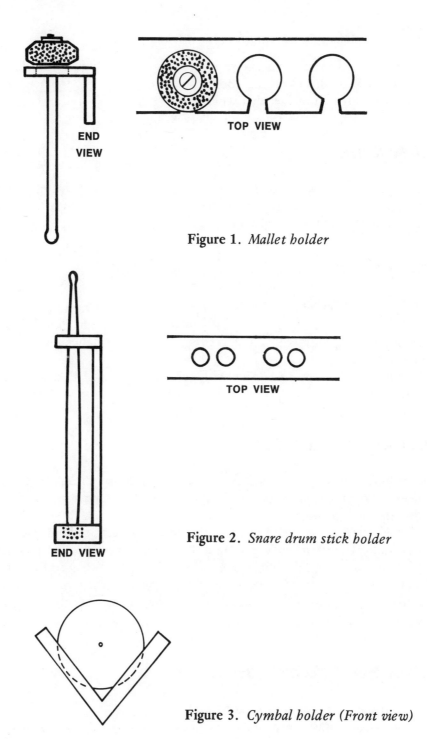

END
VIEW

TOP VIEW

Figure 1. *Mallet holder*

END VIEW

TOP VIEW

Figure 2. *Snare drum stick holder*

Figure 3. *Cymbal holder (Front view)*

Setting Up

Many punctured snare heads and stretched snares are caused by careless place-ment of the snare drums on the stand. A word of caution to the percussion players will often eliminate such accidents.

Hardware

Light petroleum grease or mutton tallow should be used on the **tension rod** threads. Household oil should be placed periodically on the moving parts of the snare strainer to assure smooth operation.

Shell

Mahogany shells should be cleaned and polished like fine furniture. A combina-tion cleaner and wax, used occasionally, will help maintain a "new" look. A scratch remover polish will help cover the nicks and scratches that inevitably come with use.

   Plastic shells may be cleaned with kerosene, cleaning wax, or any mild, non-abrasive cleaner.

Mallet Instruments

The polished metal areas (including the **bars**) on glockenspiels, orchestra bells, chimes, xylophones, marimbas, and vibraphones should be wiped with a treated cloth after each handling.

   Periodic dusting with a soft paintbrush will prevent the buildup of dust in inaccessible places, particularly around the **grommets** on glockenspiel bars.

   The bearing areas on vibraphones should be oiled periodically, according to frequency of use, with a light household oil or whatever is recommended by the manufacturer. Broken drive belts and burned-out motors are the result of in-adequate oiling procedures.

Drumhead Cleaning

Plastic drumheads should be cleaned with soap and water. Clean calfskin heads with an art gum eraser. A paintbrush can be used to remove dust from around the hoops.

Accessories

Moving parts on the damper mechanism of chimes, the hi-hat, bass drum, and the casters on movable percussions should be oiled periodically for longer life and proper operation.

NOTE: Do not oil or grease any part of the timpani unless specified by the manufacturer.

SPECIFIC PRECAUTIONS

1. Do not lay a woodwind instrument on its keys.

2. Remove the bocal when carrying an assembled bassoon.

3. Avoid storing wooden instruments in attics, basements, or automobile trunks.

4. Always place a reed cap over the clarinet or saxophone mouthpiece when the instrument is not being played.

5. Hold the saxophone by the bell when inserting a tight neckpipe, to prevent bending the keys (Figure 110, page 188).

6. Always hold a trombone when it is uncased. Do not set it on a chair or lay it on the floor.

7. Always remove the sousaphone neckpipe after playing.

8. Do not lay a sousaphone on its bell without removing the neckpipe.

ASSEMBLING THE WOODWINDS

Piccolo—Flute

1. Hold the head joint firmly.

2. Grip the main body near the tenon **socket** (Figures 4 and 5) so that no strain is placed on the **hinge rods** and tubings.

3. Insert the tenon with a twisting motion.

4. Hold the foot joint so that the fingers are arched over the hinge rod (Figure 6).

5. While holding the flute body near the tenon socket, push the foot joint on with a slight twist.

Figure 4.
Assembling the piccolo

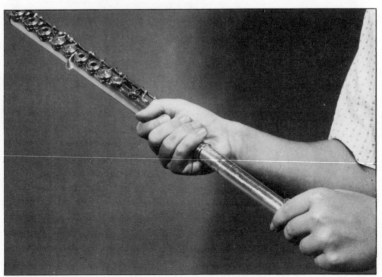

Figure 5. *Inserting the flute head joint*

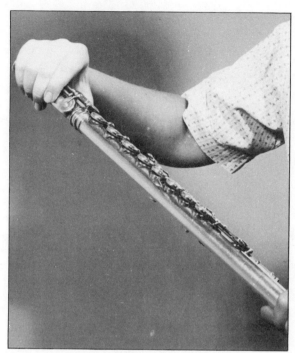

Figure 6.
Assembling the flute foot joint

Oboe—English Horn

In each step of assembling the oboe and English horn, grip the joints so that pressure exists only between the palm and the fingertips, with the fingers arched over the hinge rods. Push into position with a slight twisting motion. Carefully avoid damage to the bridge keys and **spatulas**.

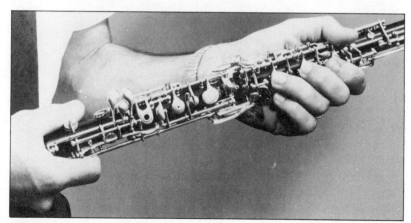

Figure 7. *Step 1, Oboe*

Figure 8. *Step 1, English horn*

Close the low B$^\flat$ key with the thumb when assembling the oboe bell (Figure 9).

Figure 9. *Step 2, Oboe*

Figure 10. *Step 2, English horn*

With the thumb and first finger on the top edge of the cork, push and twist the reed and bocal into position (Figures 11 and 12).

Figure 11. *Step 3, Oboe*

Figure 12. *Step 3, English horn*

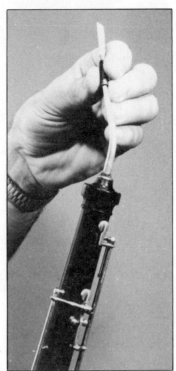

Figure 13.
Step 4, English horn

Bassoon

1. Set the boot joint on a chair, table, or on the floor.

2. With the right hand, hold the boot joint so that no pressure is exerted on the hinge rods.

3. Insert the tenor and bass joints together (Figure 14), part way into the sockets. (Bassoons equipped with locking devices should be locked during this step.)

4. Unlock the tenor and bass joints.

5. With the first finger (left hand) hooked over the bocal socket, *push* the tenor joint into position.

6. While holding the bass joint by the upper tenon, *push* the bass joint into position. Use caution to avoid key damage.

7. Hold the low B♭ key with the thumb (Figure 15) and *push* the bell onto the bass joint.

8. Hold the bocal as shown in Figure 16. Push and twist it into alignment with the **whisper key**.

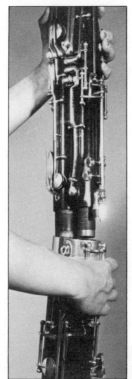

Figure 15.
Step 2, Bassoon

Figure 14. *Step 1, Bassoon*

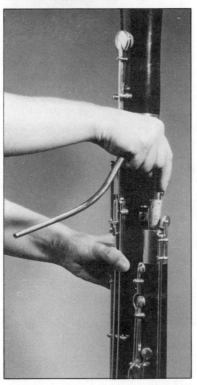

Figure 16. *Step 3, Bassoon*

Soprano Clarinets

1. Upper and lower joints
   a) Grip the upper joint with the fingers pressing the ring keys.
   b) Hold the lower joint so that needed pressure is applied only to the body and the large pad cups.
   c) Connect the joints with a twisting motion.

2. Bell
   a) Hold the bottom joint with the fingers arched over the ring key hinge rod.
   b) Place the bell on the tenon with a series of twists.

3. Barrel joint
   a) Hold the upper joint with body and ring key pressure.
   b) Place the barrel joint on the tenon with a twist.

4. Mouthpiece
   Hold the upper joint as in 3-a above. Insert the mouthpiece with a twist.

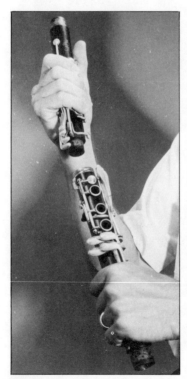

Figure 17.
Step 1, Soprano clarinet

Figure 18.
Step 2, Soprano clarinet

Figure 19.
Step 3, Soprano clarinet

5. Reed
   Install as shown in Figure 21.

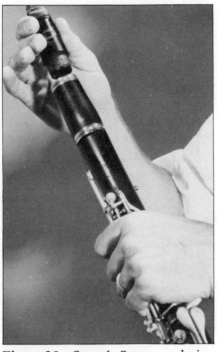

Figure 20. *Step 4, Soprano clarinet*

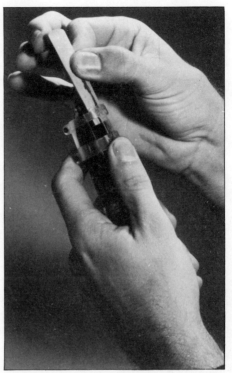

Figure 21. *Step 5, Soprano clarinet*

Alto and Bass Clarinets

1. Upper and lower joints
   a) Hold the upper joint with the fingers on the **plateau** keys.
   b) Grip the lower joint below the spatulas with the hand arched over the hinge rods.
   c) Connect the tenons with a slight twist, using caution to prevent **bridge key** damage.

2. Bell
   a) Hold the bell bow in the palm of the hand, with the fingers holding the low $E^\flat$ pad closed.
   b) Place the bell on the tenon with a twist, and align the bridge keys.

3. Neckpipe
   a) Grip the neckpipe by the bow nearest the tenon.

76— 1278

C. C. HARDY LIBRARY
ATLANTIC CHRISTIAN COLLEGE
WILSON, N. C. 27893

b) Insert the tenon in the upper joint socket, and align the octave bridge.

4. Mouthpiece
   a) Hold the neckpipe near the socket, with the heel of the hand braced against the upper joint.
   b) Insert the mouthpiece.

Figure 22.
Step 1, Large clarinet

Figure 23.
Step 2, Large clarinet

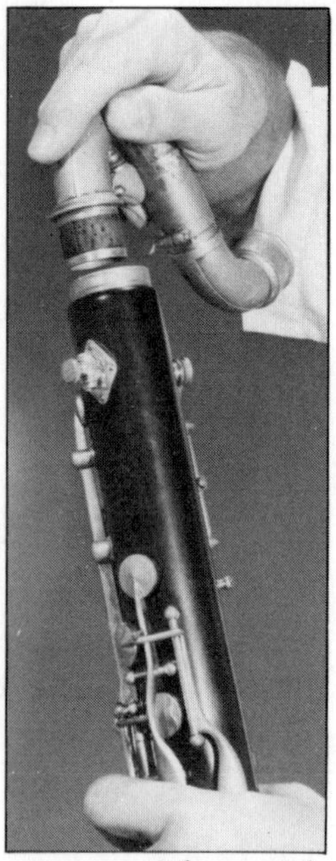

Figure 24.
Step 3, Large clarinet

Figure 25.
Step 4, Large clarinet

Inspections 2

The following procedures may seem intricate and time-consuming, yet one inspection will convince the director or instrumentalist of the importance of maintaining thorough, periodic inspections.

To test *properly* for instrument leakage, it is necessary for the director to place his mouth on many instruments to create a vacuum. It is advisable, therefore, to begin the inspection with clean cloths and an antiseptic solution for sterilization. On *unlacquered* instruments (oboes, clarinets, flutes), alcohol is quite effective. For other equipment, see the ''Standard Repairs'' chapter.

Although instrument malfunctions have a variety of causes, the testing procedures listed in this chapter should pinpoint the source of a majority of the problems and guide the director to the proper solutions.

After each instrument is inspected visually and physically (as in the following procedures), it should be checked by playing with all fingering combinations.

NOTE: Woodwind key openings vary according to the instrument, the brand, and the model. The best guide to follow is to determine, visually, if one or more keys open further than the others, and if a **foot** cork is missing. Then physically check for slack action and, if a bridge key, for simultaneous pad **seatings** with a **feeler** or **leak light**. On many saxophones the lower stack pads and the G pad open too widely, causing intonation problems and excessive finger movements. A visual and physical check will expose this problem quickly.

PICCOLO—FLUTE

Visual Inspection

    1.   Check the **tuning cork** for proper setting (Figure 26).

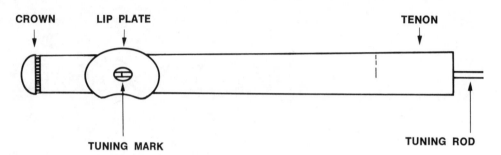

Figure 26. *Flute tuning*

    2.   Check for a loose or missing **crown.**

    3.   Check for severe dents on all joints.

    4.   Check for accumulated dust or oil around keys and posts.

    5.   Check the **blow hole** for cleanliness.

    6.   Check the bore for dirt accumulation.

    7.   Check all pads to see if skins are moth-eaten or frayed.

    8.   Check for missing **pad screws** or **pad washers.**

    9.   Check for bent keys.

  10.   Check to see if all keys open the same distance from the tone holes.

  11.   Check the case hardware (hinges and latch) for security.

  12.   Check for presence of a tuning rod and swab.

  13.   Check the case interior for cleanliness.

  14.   Check for loose **pivot screws** and **hinge rods.**

Physical Inspection

    1.   Check the head and foot joint tenons for snug fits.

2. Check all keys for proper functioning:
   a) Does the thumb B♭ key close the thumb pad and the B♭ key simultaneously?
   b) Does the forked B♭ (first finger, right hand) key close the F, F♯, and B♭ keys simultaneously?
   c) Do the D and E keys close simultaneously with the F♯?
   d) Does the low C lever close the C♯ and C pads simultaneously?
   e) Is there a slack motion in any bridge key before it actuates its relative key?
   f) Is there a metallic sound when the keys are operated?
   g) Do all keys operate freely?
   h) Do the pads stick?

3. Check for loose action of hinge rods and **hinge tubings**.

4. Check the head joint for leaks:
   a) After cleaning the **lip plate** and blow hole, place the palm of one hand over the open tenon.
   b) Place the lips over the lip plate and create a vacuum by sucking until portions of the lips are pulled into the blow hole. If the vacuum holds for at least fifteen seconds without releasing any pressure, there are no serious leaks. Leaks are present if there is a release of pressure during the fifteen seconds.
   c) To determine whether the leaks are in the tuning cork or in the solder around the lip plate, remove the crown and push the tuning cork out of the *opposite end* (see Figure 57, page 78) with the **tuning rod**.
   d) Cover the ends (which are now open) with both palms and again create a vacuum as in the preceding manner. If no leaks are present, the tuning cork is the source of the leak. If a leak is still present, the leak is around the soldered portion of the lip plate. Only an experienced repairman should resolder the lip plate.

5. Check the body for leaks:
   a) Place a cork stopper in the foot tenon.
   b) Lightly cover the keys as in fingering low D.
   c) Place the lips on the head joint socket and create a vacuum.
   d) If the vacuum does not hold, a leak is present. The seriousness of the leak can be determined by the speed of the vacuum release. Inability to create a vacuum is an indication of one or more serious leaks. Follow the repair procedures listed in the "Standard Repairs" chapter.
   e) Blow lightly into the body part to check for weak springs.

6. Check the foot joint for leaks:
   a) Hold the palm of one hand over the bottom end.

b) Lightly close the low C key.

c) Create a vacuum with the mouth on the tenon end.

d) Follow the same procedures as in item 5-d and e above.

NOTE: When all standard methods of locating a leak have failed (using a feeler, leak light, removing the key and inspecting the pad, checking spring tensions, etc.), a sure and quick means of finding a leak is by smoke testing. Although the smoke residue on the pads will be offensive for a brief period afterward, this method will reveal leaks around posts, octave tubes, tenons, and sockets, cracks in the body, unsoldered tone holes, and even in new pads—which sometimes have coarse, open pores in the pad skins. When working alone, a large mirror will be helpful in locating leaks that are not in the visual range of the tester. Following the test, the instrument should be swabbed with alcohol, bore oil (wooden instruments only), or mouthwash to eliminate as much odor as possible.

OBOE—ENGLISH HORN

Visual Inspection

1. Check the reed for chips, cracks, opening, and strength.

2. Check all tenons for chipped areas and frayed tenon corks.

3. Check all body parts for cracks.

4. Check for dust and oil around keys and posts.

5. Check for worn or frayed skin pads.

6. Check the bore of all body parts for cleanliness.

7. Check the automatic octave keys for proper operation.

8. Check all keys for proper opening from tone holes.

9. Check for bent or broken keys.

10. Check the case hardware for security.

11. Check for cleaning swabs, cork grease, and tenon caps.

12. Check the case interior for cleanliness.

13. Check the tone holes:
    a) Are they dirty?
    b) Are they chipped?

14. Check the English horn bocals:
    a) Do they need new cork?
    b) Are they dirty or damaged?

15. Check for loose pivot screws and hinge rods.

Physical Inspection

1. Check all keys for proper functioning:
   a) Do all bridge keys close their related pads?
   b) Do the keys respond quickly, or are they sluggish?
   c) Is the inaction of a key caused by a broken or unhooked **needle spring?**
   d) Is there unnecessary noise caused by missing key corks?
   e) Is the sluggish action of a key caused by a loose or twisted post?

2. Check for loose **tenon rings.**

3. Check for leaks in the upper joint:
   a) Place a stopper in the tenon end.
   b) Place the fingers over the keys as though fingering G.
   c) Place the mouth over the reed socket and create a vacuum.
   d) Follow the previously mentioned techniques (Flute, Physical Inspection, pages 29 and 30) for determining the presence and location of leaks.

4. Check for leaks in the lower joint:
   a) Place a stopper in the *middle* tenon socket.
   b) Using both hands, lightly close the keys as though fingering low B♭ .
   c) Place the mouth over (or in) the bell tenon and create a vacuum.
   d) Follow the standard leak-finding procedures.

5. Check the tenons for snug fits.

6. Check the thumb rest for cork and tightness.

CLARINETS

Visual Inspection

1. Check the mouthpiece:
   a) Are there nicked or chipped areas on the **rails** or the tip?

  b) Is it clean?
  c) Does the ligature fit properly?
  d) Is the reed chipped, cracked, or extremely weak?
  e) Is the cork satisfactory?

2. Check the body parts for cracks.

3. Check all tenons for frayed corks and chipped areas.

4. Check the tone holes:
  a) Are they chipped?
  b) Are they dirty?

5. Check the bores for evidence of improper swabbing.

6. Check for loose pivot screws and hinge rods.

7. Check for cleanliness around posts and keys.

8. Check for broken or bent keys.

9. Check for frayed or moth-eaten pads.

10. Check all keys for proper opening.

11. Check the alto and bass clarinet bell:
  a) Does the low E♭ (bell key) close simultaneously with low E and F?
  b) Are there serious dents in the bell bow?
  c) Is the bell bow brace unsoldered?
  d) Is the low E♭ key corked to prevent bridge key noises?

12. Check the case hinges and latches for proper security.

13. Check the case for swabs, cork grease, and mouthpiece cap.

14. Check the case for cleanliness.

Physical Inspection

1. Check all bridge keys for proper operation:
  a) Is there loose action between A and A♭ (G♯)?
  b) Does the forked E♭-B♭ fingering close the upper joint pad properly?
  c) Is there loose play between the low F **presser foot** and the low E and F♯ spatula?
  d) Can the clarinet slur from a fourth line D to the third line B without squeaking?

2. Check all joints for snug fits.

3. Check all keys for fast response.

4. Check the tenon and **bell rings** for tightness.

5. Check the upper joint for leaks:
   a) Place the palm of the right hand over the middle tenon.
   b) Finger middle C.
   c) Place the lips in the upper tenon and create a vacuum.
   d) Follow the procedure mentioned previously for locating leaks (Flute, Physical Inspection, pages 29 and 30).

6. Check the lower joint for leaks:
   a) Place the palm of the left hand over the bell tenon.
   b) Finger low E.
   c) Place the mouth on the middle tenon socket and create a vacuum.
   d) Follow the normal leak-finding procedure.

7. Check the bass and contrabass clarinets for leaks. Using a leak light, check the upper joint as follows:
   a) Check the closed keys (A, A$\flat$, chromatic E$\flat$-B$\flat$, C$\sharp$-G$\sharp$, and the four side keys).
   b) Depress the thumb key and check it and its relative key (opposite side of the body) for simultaneous closings.
   c) Check each finger key and its relative key as in b) above.
   d) If the octave or register key(s) are too small to emit light, they should be checked for proper closing with a feeler.
   e) Follow the procedures in the "Standard Repairs" chapter for reseating or replacing leaking pads.

8. Check the lower joint on the bass and contrabass clarinets with a leak light as follows:
   a) Check the closed pads (F$\sharp$-B trill, low F$\sharp$, and low G$\sharp$).
   b) Check the main line or stack pads.
   c) Check the bridge keys for simultaneous closings.
   d) Follow the standard repair procedures to eliminate leaks.

9. Check all keys for proper corking.

10. Check all pads for looseness.

NOTE: Using a pencil-shaped typewriter eraser (with a pointed end), lightly touch each pad on both the front and back sides to see if the pad will fall out. This procedure will often eliminate the annoying loose pad problems that seemingly occur prior to every concert!

BASSOONS

Visual Inspection

1. Check the reeds for splitting or chipping.

2. Check the bocals:
   a) Are they properly corked?
   b) Are they dirty?
   c) Are they bent or damaged?
   d) Are the **nibs** stopped up? (To prevent nib damage, use only a thin, nonmetallic straw or bristle when cleaning the hole.)

3. Check for bent or broken keys.

4. Check the joint lock for security:
   a) Are its screws loose?
   b) Is it bent or broken?

5. Check the crutch and crutch holder for looseness.

6. Check for loose pivot screws or hinge rods.

7. Check for frayed or loose pads.

8. Check the tone holes for dents or chipped areas.

9. Check all bores for improper swabbing.

10. Check the end **bow** for evidences of leaks around the **flange**. (The **bow cap** can usually be removed easily with a slight pressure.)

11. Check for dirt and excessive oil around the posts and keys.

12. Check all tenons:
    a) Are the corks worn or loose?
    b) Are there chipped areas?

13. Check the case hardware for security.

14. Check the case for the presence of cork grease, swabs, and strap.

15. Check the case for cleanliness.

Physical Inspection

1. Check all keys for proper functioning:
   a) Do all bridge mechanisms operate in unison?

      b) Do the keys respond freely?
      c) Are there unnecessary noises?
      d) Is there slack in bridge keys before response?
      e) Are there broken or unhooked springs?
      f) Do the keys open the proper distance from tone holes?
      g) Does the whisper key function properly?

2. Check all tenons for snug fit.

3. Check for loose pads. (Follow the procedure as described for clarinets.)

4. Check the tenon rings or bands for looseness.

5. Check the tenor joint for leaks:
      a) Place a stopper in the bocal socket.
      b) Using both hands, close all keys.
      c) Place the mouth in the tenon and create a vacuum.
      d) For finding leaks in the bassoon, the leak light and feeler must be used jointly. This is due to the shape of some tone holes, key guards, and the varying size of the bore.

6. Check the **butt** or boot joint for leaks:
      a) Place a stopper in one of the tenon sockets.
      b) Close the keys.
      c) Place the mouth in the other tenon socket and create a vacuum.
      d) Follow the standard leak-finding procedures.

7. Check the bass joint for leaks. Follow procedure as in items 5 and 6 above.

NOTE: Due to the nature of the wood, the texture of the pad skins, and the size of the bassoon, it is difficult to form a tight vacuum.

8. Check the bell joint for leaks (leak light testing).

SAXOPHONES

Visual Inspection

1. Check the mouthpiece:
      a) Is it clean?
      b) Is it cracked on the tenon end? (An indication of improper corking.)

    c) Are the rails and the tip dented or chipped?
    d) Does the ligature fit properly?
    e) Is the reed in good condition?

2. Check the neckpipe:
    a) Is it corked properly?
    b) Is it dirty inside?
    c) Is the octave pad skin eaten away by saliva acids?
    d) Is the tenon warped or dented?
    e) Is the hinge rod loose?

3. Check the body:
    a) Are there serious dents?
    b) Is there evidence of poor swabbing? Green stains inside the bell bow and dark, dried, or brittle low D♯ (E♭) pad indicate improper drying.

4. Check for bent or broken keys.

5. Check for proper key opening.

6. Check for dark or frayed pads.

7. Check the case hardware for security.

8. Check the case for swabs, mouthpiece cap, end plug, and a sturdy accessory compartment.

9. Check the case for cleanliness.

10. Check for loose pivot screws and hinge rods.

11. Check for loose bell-to-body brace.

12. Check for loose or missing key guards.

Physical Inspection

1. Check all keys:
    a) Do all keys respond freely?
    b) Do the bridge keys operate in unison?
    c) Is there slack motion in the bridge keys?
    d) Do the key rollers on the **table keys** operate freely?

2. Check for loose pads. Use an eraser as in clarinet pad-testing.

3. Check all pads for leaks:
    a) Using a leak light, check all closed pads starting with the upper (palm) F.

b) Check the upper stack pads and their relative bridge keys for simultaneous closings.

c) Check the lower stack and low C pads.

d) Check the bridge mechanisms as in (b) above. In particular, finger F while fingering G$\sharp$, and check both pads for leaks.

e) Check the bell keys and their proper bridge functionings.

NOTE: To test for leaks in the baritone or bass saxophone, the side B$\flat$ key must be removed and the leak light inserted through the B$\flat$ tone hole. The low C or the low D$\sharp$ key must then be removed for checking the side B$\flat$ pad.

4. Check the octave mechanism:
   a) Finger G above the staff.
      Is the low octave key open and the neck octave key closed?
   b) Finger A above the staff.
      Does the neck octave open and the low octave close?

PISTON VALVE INSTRUMENTS

Visual Inspection

1. Check the mouthpiece:
   a) Does it need replating?
   b) Is the **shank** bent or oval-shaped?
   c) Is the throat clean and free from obstruction?
   d) Are there dents in the rim?

2. Check for serious dents.

3. Check for loose braces.

4. Check the valve **ports** and tuning slide interiors for evidence of improper cleaning.

5. Check for missing **finger buttons**, **pull knobs**, bottom valve caps, **finger hooks**, lyre holders, lyre screws, and **water keys**.

6. Check for misshaped **thumb rings**, **finger rings**, and finger hooks.

7. Check the case hardware for security.

8. Check the case interior for a sturdy accessory compartment and cleanliness.

9. Check the case compartment for valve oil, slide grease, lyre, and a chamois skin.

10. Check the sousaphone neckpipe, gooseneck, and tuning bits for damage.

11. Check the sousaphone and other adjustable bell brasses for loose or missing **bell spuds** and **bell screws.**

12. Check the pistons:
    a) Broad worn spots indicate oval-shaped casings.
    b) A thin worn line indicates a dent in the casing.
    c) Flaking or peeling of the piston finish indicates poor plating.
    d) A tarnished piston indicates use of saliva as a lubricant.

13. Check the finger buttons for even alignment.

14. Check the piston alignment by determining whether the indented ring marks on the piston stems are level with the tops of the upper valve caps (Figure 76, page 108).

15. Check the water key corks.

Physical Inspection

1. Check all slides for ease of removal.

2. Check the valves for spring tension and fast response.

3. Check the top and bottom valve caps for easy removal.

4. Check suspected leaks by stopping one end of the tube and forcing air pressure into the other end.

5. Check water key springs for proper tension.

ROTARY VALVE INSTRUMENTS

Visual Inspection

1. Check the mouthpiece as in the Piston Valve Instruments section.

2. Check for severe dents.

3. Check for loose braces.

4. Check the slide interiors for improper cleaning.

5. Check the alignment of each valve port:
    a) Remove the bottom valve cap.
    b) Locate the alignment mark at the end of the rotor shaft (Figure 27).
    c) Depress and release the valve key to determine if the marks on the shaft align with the mark on the bearing washer.

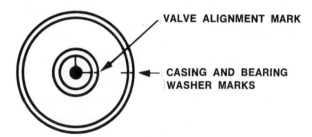

Figure 27. *Aligning the rotary valve*

6. Check for alignment of keys or levers.

7. Check the case hardware for security.

8. Check the case interior:
    a) Is there a sturdy strap?
    b) Are there loose articles?
    c) Is it clean?

9. Check the valve strings for wear and for proper size and type.

10. Check for missing finger hook, **pull rings**, lyre holders, and lyre screws.

Physical Inspection

1. Check all slides for ease of removal.

2. Check all valves for correct spring tension and quick response.

3. Check the valve action for slack in the strings.

4. Check the valve action for unnecessary noise.

TROMBONE

Visual Inspection

1. Check the mouthpiece as in the Piston Valve Instruments section.

2. Check for proper cleanliness:
   a) Remove the inner slides and sight through each bore.
   b) Pull the tuning slide and inspect the tubing interior.

3. Check the water key cork.

4. Check for bad dents in the bell, bell tubing, tuning slide, and hand slide bow.

5. Check the case hardware for security.

6. Check the case interior:
   a) Are the turnbuttons or straps in good condition?
   b) Is the accessory compartment in good condition?
   c) Is the case clean?
   d) Are the lyre and cleaning rod holding mechanisms adequate to prevent them from coming loose in the case?

7. Check the stockings for signs of improper cleaning procedures (accumulation of deposits), and for improper slide alignment (worn spots).

Physical Inspection

1. Check the tuning slide for easy removal.

2. Check the hand slide for smooth action:
   a) Before assembling, place the slides vertically with the slide bow resting on the floor.
   b) Slowly lift the inner slides to check for dents or rough spots.
   c) Place the slides in playing position. Release the hand slide and see if gravity will move it to the sixth or seventh position.

3. Check the hand slide for compression:
   a) Hold the slide vertically with the open ends down.
   b) Lift the hand slide up to sixth or seventh position.
   c) Stop both openings of the inner tubings.
   d) Release the hand slide. A tight slide will require several seconds for gravity to bring it to first position. A loose or leaking slide will descend much more rapidly. Loss of compression is some-

times caused by a poor water key cork or a weak water key spring. This can be further checked by removing the inner slide, closing one end of the hand slide, and blowing into the other end.

4. Check for adequate slide bumper corks by lightly bumping the hand slide to first position.

5. Check the slide lock for a secure fit.

DRUMS

Visual Inspection

1. Check the batter and snare heads for holes, breaks, and cleanliness.
2. Check the shell and metallic parts for evidences of improper care (dents, scratches, rust, and dirt).
3. Check the hoops for even or level installation.
4. Check the snares for correct size and placement on the head.
5. Check for dust accumulation around the hoop.
6. Check for missing tension rods and broken strainer parts.
7. Check for proper greasing of tension rods.
8. Check for stretched or broken snare strands.
9. Check for frayed or broken snare attachment cords.

Physical Inspection

1. Check the snare strainer for smooth operation.
2. Check the snare strainer for correct pressure and release.
3. Check the head tension at each tension rod.

TIMPANI

Visual Inspection

1. Check for severe dents in the shell.

2. Check for missing or broken tension rods.

3. Check the head for cleanliness.

4. Check the head for breaks.

5. Check the head for a proper collar and even (level) application of tension by all rods.

6. Check the tension rods for greasing.
    (See NOTE: Chapter 1, Percussions, Accessories, page 17.)

Physical Inspection

1. Check the pedal for proper tension, release, and holding.

2. Check for unnecessary noises when the pedal is operated.

3. Check the casters for proper operation.

MALLET INSTRUMENTS

Visual Inspection

1. Check each instrument for dust accumulation and filmy deposits on bars and tubes.

2. Check for loose bars caused by worn grommets or a broken bar-retaining cord.

3. Check for broken, bent, or disconnected damper mechanisms.

4. Check the resonating tubes for dents and cracks.

Physical Inspection

1. Check the pulsators (on vibes) for free action. (Bent pulsator rods, improper oiling, and dirt accumulation will often cause irregular pulsations.)

2. Check the resonator speed controls, drive belts, and pulleys for proper functioning. A frayed or stretched belt, a loose pulley, or a burned-out rheostat can also cause irregular pulsations.

3. Check the casters for free, rolling actions. Accumulations of lint, dust, loose strands from floor mops, etc., often become wound around the axle of the casters.

4. Check each bar individually for correct musical response. (Worn grommets on bell lyras can cause a metallic rattle. Slack in the bar-retaining cord can muffle the marimba notes.)

CYMBALS AND GONGS

Visual and Physical Inspection

1. Check for cracks (see the "Standard Repairs" chapter for repairs).

2. Check the cymbal holders and gong support cord:
   a) Are they worn or frayed?
   b) Do they prevent a clear response?

3. Check the gong stand for rigidity.

4. Check for proper storage and handling.

PERCUSSION ACCESSORIES

Visual and Physical Inspection

1. Check all small accessories (wood blocks, tambourines, etc.) for broken parts.

2. Check the snare and bass drum stands:
   a) Is it good, sturdy equipment that is not likely to collapse?
   b) Are the threads stripped on the tightening screws?
   c) Are the rubber crutch tips deteriorated?
   d) Are the sleeves (for snare drum stand-arms) in good condition?
   e) Do the cradle felt, screws, or other parts for the bass drum stand need replacing?

3. Check the bass drum pedal (stage band) for proper care:
   a) Is the strap worn or broken?

    b) Has it been oiled properly?

    c) Do all tension screws work properly?

    d) Is the action free?

    e) Has the beater been rotated to prevent wear on one side?

    f) Have oil and dust accumulated around the working parts?

4. Check all mallets and beaters for loose heads.

5. Check all snare drum sticks for jagged or broken tips.

Suggested Repair Equipment 3

The equipment listed in this chapter has been organized into separate sections in order of priority, to accommodate each instrumentalist's skill, his budget, and his nearness to a competent repairman.

Many items in List A should be standard equipment in *every* school that has a band program, even though repair service may be ideal. It is doubtful that any administrator would be reluctant to spend the small amount necessary to purchase repair equipment that could mean eventual savings which far exceed the initial cost. Few directors wish to lose valuable student hours due to the lack of basic items of repair equipment needed for emergencies.

Each succeeding section (B through E) presupposes that the director has purchased the tools and equipment listed in previous sections, and that he is qualified to proceed with more difficult repairs.

To determine the current price for each item and to become familiar with the tools and equipment, the director should consult one or more of the repair supply catalogs listed in the bibliography.

Most instrumentalists, with a little manual skill, can make many of the tools, but the time required to make them does not justify the effort. The only possible exception is the feelers, which can be made of wooden matches and a thin strip of cellophane (i.e., a cigarette band), and the assembly (or mounting) boards.

LIST A:

First Priority Tools and Supplies

Tools

1. One mouthpiece puller, preferably with various sized collars (see Figure 72, page 102)

2. One clarinet screwdriver, preferably with swivel top, a six-inch blade, and a short reversible blade

3. One saxophone screwdriver (Figure 56, page 75)

4. One pad slick (Figure 34, page 57)

5. One bunsen burner (an alcohol burner is not as satisfactory)

6. One pair of six-inch, flat nose pliers (smooth jaws)

7. A one-inch rawhide mallet (Figure 75, page 106)

8. A *good* four-inch vise

9. Three feelers (Figure 32, page 57)

10. One cornet-trumpet mandrel for holding instruments in the vise while performing repairs (Figure 130, page 200)

11. A flexible trombone cleaning brush, which can be used for *all* brass instruments

12. One mouthpiece brush (woodwinds)

13. One mouthpiece brush (brasses)

14. A set of testing corks

15. One spring hook

16. One clarinet assembly board (Figure 114, page 190)

17. One pin vise

Supplies

1. One can of penetrating oil
2. A tube of liquid shellac
3. One hundred assorted, tapered water key corks
4. One hundred assorted felt washers
5. One hundred assorted cork washers
6. One dozen 3/16″ × 1-1/2″ French horn corks
7. One hundred assorted, double skin and beveled, medium thickness clarinet pads (these can also be used for piccolo, oboe, and flute (small pads only) in an emergency)
8. One jar of mutton tallow (see Mutton Tallow in the "Terminology" chapter)
9. One hundred assorted saxophone (felt) key bumpers
10. One hundred assorted saxophone key felts
11. One hundred silencer skins (for left-hand levers on clarinets)
12. One spool of French horn valve cord (twenty-pound linen line)
13. Six feet of cord for attaching snares onto drums
14. One can of nonabrasive brass polish
15. An assortment of rags
16. Two single-edged razor blades or a sharp knife
17. One package of paper for cleaning eyeglasses
18. One bottle of alcohol or a good disinfectant
19. One package of pipe cleaners
20. Six sticks of white pad cement
21. One dozen thumb-rest screws
22. One bottle of key oil

LIST B:

Select from This List After the Purchase of List A Tools and Supplies

Tools

1. Leak light

2. One set of wedges for removing stuck trombone tapers (Figure 82, page 115)

3. One valve mirror (Figure 77, page 108)

4. One bench knife

5. One pair of six-inch, round nose pliers (Figures 73 and 74, pages 103 and 104)

6. One set of key leveling wedges for saxophones (Figure 113, page 189)

7. One saxophone assembly board (Figure 126, page 198)

8. One set of tone hole reamers for removing chipped tone holes on clarinets

9. One hooked scraper for removing old joint cork

10. One straight scraper for cleaning shellac from grooves in tenons

11. One valve cleaning rod

12. One emory stone

13. One shellac spatula (Figure 43, page 64)

Supplies

1. One hundred assorted saxophone pads

2. Four sheets of fine garnet paper

3. Four shellac sticks

4. One sheet of 1/8-inch cork

5. One assortment of key cork

6. One bottle of contact cement

7. One small bottle of powdered pumice

8. Two sheets of extra fine waterproof abrasive paper

LIST C:

To Be Purchased Only After the Skills Required for Lists A and B Have Been Developed

Tools

1. One jeweler's anvil

2. One tenon expander, can opener type (Figure 58, page 79, and Figure 61, page 93)

3. One set of saxophone key bending tools (Figure 113, page 189)

4. One 1/2-inch (.5000) trombone slide mandrel (for removing dents in trombone slides)

5. One flute key opening gauge

6. One dent hammer (small)

7. One cork protector, for recorking saxophone necks (Figure 66, page 96)

8. One assembly board for flutes (Figure 114, page 190)

9. One pair of needle spring pliers, for removing whole needle springs (Figure 46, page 65)

10. One vernier caliper

11. One flute head joint expander (Figure 59, page 81)

12. One six-inch mill file

13. One pair of common slip-joint pliers

Supplies

1. Six flute **tuning corks**

2. One dozen straight saxophone neck corks (eight for the alto, four for the tenor and baritone)

3. One dozen post shims

4. One hundred assorted flat springs (clarinet)

5. One hundred assorted flat springs (saxophones)

6. One dozen flat spring screws

7. Three feet of heavy cotton cord

8. One foot of .025 flute spring wire

9. Six piccolo head corks

LIST D:

Adequate Time Must Be Allowed for the Use of Items in This List

Tools

1. One pair of six-inch diagonal cutters (Figure 47, **page 66**)

2. One pair of needle spring pliers for removing broken needle springs (Figure 45, **page 65**)

3. One tone hole file (Figure 69, **page 97**)

4. One awl

5. One jeweler's saw frame (Figure 55, **page 74**)

6. One dozen jeweler's saw blades

7. One oboe assembly board (Figure 116, **page 192**)

8. One dozen flute pad clamps (Figure 36, **page 59**)

Supplies

1. An assortment of clarinet and saxophone pivot screws. Since sizes vary according to instrument type and brand, the director will be wise to order only a dozen for each of the brands that are popular in his area.

2. One hundred assorted needle springs

3. Four dozen assorted water key springs (one dozen each of the four most popular sizes)

4. One hundred assorted double skin flute pads

5. One hundred thin, flute pad washers (twenty-five of each size: 16, 17, 18, and 19 mm)

LIST E:

This List Should Be Considered Only by Instrumentalists to Whom Repair Facilities Are Not Accessible, Or Who Have Unusual Mechanical Ability

Tools

1. One set pivot screw reamers (Figure 53, page 72)

2. One set post reamers (Figure 52, page 71)

3. One set hinge tube shorteners (Figure 54, page 72)

4. One hand mandrel (flute)

5. One body mandrel (flute)

6. One 1/2″ × 30″ tapered mandrel (for removing dents in cornet, trumpet, and trombone bell tubing)

7. One bassoon assembly board (Figure 120, page 194)

8. One 21/32″ to 23/32″ expandable reamer (for removing dents from cornet casings)

9. One trombone bumper cork remover (Figure 92, page 121)

10. One set of number drills, 1 through 60

11. One hand or electric drill

Supplies

1. One hundred assorted oboe pads

2. One hundred assorted pads for alto and bass clarinets and bassoon

3. One fifteen-inch piece of **key roller** tubing for saxophone keys

4. One set of ebony compound and solvent

5. One sheet of 3/32″ × 4″ × 12″ cork

Persons who desire to learn more about soldering, drilling, polishing, burnishing, major dent work, crack pinning, swedging, and lathe work should consult their local repairman for assistance. Such techniques cannot be described easily, and the equipment is quite expensive.

Standard Repairs 4

Inexperienced instrumentalists are prone to make mistakes in their first repair attempts. This is due, primarily, to such factors as the variety of structural weaknesses in each instrument, its age, its brand, its type, and the care it has received. It is doubtful, however, whether anyone who follows safe repair practices could cause irreparable damage to any instrument. It is probable that he will receive genuine satisfaction from a successful repair attempt.

The problems enumerated in this chapter are the ones encountered by the average director. While some directors will have difficulties with the simplest repairs, others will be able to follow the most difficult procedures. Each director, therefore, must judge for himself what repairs he should attempt. The following points should be considered before making this decision:

1. The actual need (distance to a reliable repairman, band budget, etc.)

2. Time

3. Personal interest

4. Dexterity (this can be developed if the interest is strong)

5. Availability of old instruments on which to practice

After each heading in this chapter, the tools and/or supplies are listed that will be necessary for the given repair. It should be mentioned again that the tools and supplies are listed in order of required proficiency, and *this order should be ignored only at the director's risk.* For instance, use of the tenon expanders might necessitate the filing away of precious metal around a flute head or foot joint, or a saxophone neck tenon, if the director has not first discovered the malleability of brass as evidenced in pulling stuck slides or bending saxophone keys for releveling pad cups. Therefore, if the director has only the tools and experience required in the A and B lists, a repair problem that requires tools from Lists D or E usually should be left to a professional repairman.

Many of the problems not listed in this chapter are covered in Chapter 5, Most Frequent Problems.

GENERAL WOODWIND PROCEDURES

Preparing Key Cork

(List B Supplies)

1. Select several thicknesses of cork and apply a thin coat of contact cement on one side of each piece.

2. Allow them to dry thoroughly (one hour) and place them in a dust-free container that will not allow the coated sides to touch.

3. When needed, the cemented side will adhere readily to a clean, heated key.

Corking Keys

(List B Tools and Supplies)

1. Scrape off the old cork.

2. Heat the area to be corked just beyond the point where it is comfortable to the touch (overheating will burn the lacquer on saxophone keys).

3. Apply the coated side of the cork (Figure 28) to the underside of the key.

4. Press the corked area against the key until cool.

5. With a razor blade or a knife, trim so that all sides are beveled (Figure 29).

6. If the cork is too thick, slip a strip of fine garnet paper (with the rough side toward the cork) under the key, depress the key lightly, and pull the garnet paper out (Figure 30). Repeat until the desired thickness is obtained.

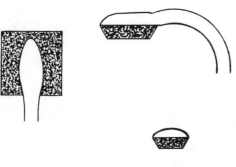

Figure 28.
*Corking the key
(Top view)*

Figure 29.
*Trimmed cork
(Side and end views)*

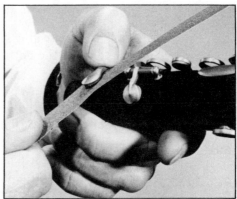

Figure 30. *Removing excess key cork*

Preparing Garnet Paper

1. Cut into 1/2–inch or 5/8–inch-wide strips that can be used for sanding tenons (Figure 42, page 63), neck corks (Figures 67 and 68, page 96), or in removing key cork (Figure 30).

2. Another helpful use of garnet paper is to glue strips of it to both sides of a thin (1/8 × 1/2 × 8-inch) slat for smoothing key cork edges. If used this way, several slats should be made at one time and kept available for immediate use.

Installing Glued Pads

(List B Tools and Supplies)

The following process includes the C key and trill keys on flutes, all pads on clarinets, oboes, bassoons, and most saxophones. Piccolo pads require special treatment.

1. Remove the key from the instrument.

2. Remove the old pad and the glue with a screwdriver.

3. Select the correct pad size.

4. Puncture the pad (Figure 31) with a needle or pin (white skin pads only) to let the heated air escape.

5. Hold the key over the flame for two or three seconds (longer for larger keys).

6. Apply the white glue stick to the inside of the cup and let enough melt to cover the bottom. A shellac stick is preferable for gluing kid skin pads.

NOTE: The white glue and shellac sticks may be heated and tapered to a point for easier application in the smaller cups.

7. While the glue is still in liquid form, press the pad in the cup. The saxophone pad should be pressed firmly into the cup by holding it level against a clean, flat surface while cooling.

8. Install the key on the instrument.

PUNCTURE HERE

Figure 31. *Puncturing the pad*

Seating Glued Pads (except for saxophones)

(List A Tools and Supplies)

1. With a feeler or leak light, locate the points of strong and weak contact of the pad against the tone hole (Figure 32).

2. Heat the pad as in Figure 33, using caution to prevent burning the pad or the instrument.

3. Shift the pad with a pad slick (Figure 34) until it contacts the tone hole evenly on all sides. It may be necessary to repeat these three steps several times before a satisfactory **covering** is obtained.

4. For shifting smaller pads, use a narrow pad slick (Figure 108, page 188) made from an old hacksaw blade.

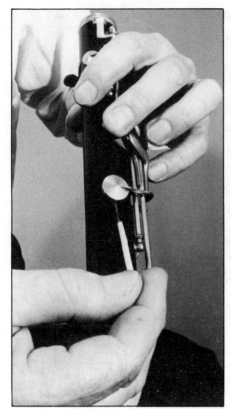

Figure 32. *Testing the pad seating*

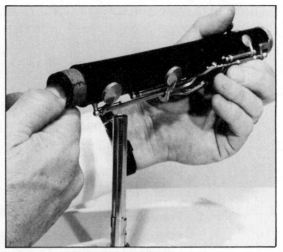

Figure 33. *Heating the mounted key*

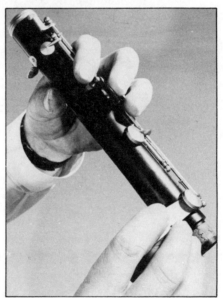

Figure 34.
Shifting the pad

Seating Glued Pads (Saxophones)

(List C Tools and Supplies)

Although several keys on the saxophone can be seated with key-leveling wedges and finger pressure (or light taps of the rawhide mallet), others such as the stack and bell keys should be leveled with the key bending tools (Figure 113, page 189) as listed in "C" tools. Body dents, bent hinge rods, and loose tone holes (soldered type) are often results of careless leveling attempts with the rawhide mallet.

1. Using the leak light, locate the strong and weak contact points of the pad.

2. Place a leveling wedge under the strong contact point (the area of the pad that touches the tone hole first).

3. Apply pressure on the weak side (Figure 35).

4. Repeat the first three steps as often as necessary to seat the pad satisfactorily.

5. For a smoother coverage after seating, wet the pad thoroughly and place a cork wedge under the key foot (to hold the pad against the tone hole), and allow several hours for drying.

6. Remove the cork wedge and test for leakage.

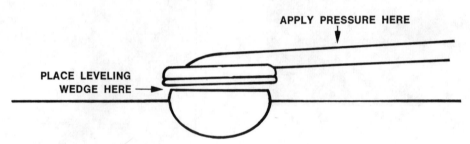

Figure 35. *Leveling the saxophone key*

Installing and Seating Flute Pads

(List D Tools and Supplies)

The following procedures are to be employed for large pads on the average, student-model flutes. Due to the intricacy of the French open hole models, the director should *not* attempt to replace leaking pads on them or to do more than make the necessary, minor adjustments.

1. Remove the key(s) from the flute. (See page 60, Flute Repad, No. 1.)

2. Unscrew the pad screw(s) or remove the booster (Figure 107, page 187).

3. With a needle or small screwdriver, remove the old pad(s) and paper washer(s) (**shims**).

4. Insert a new pad, but do not insert the paper shims.

5. Attach the metal washer and the pad screw, or the tone booster.

6. Install the key on the flute.

7. Using the feeler, test for strong and weak contact points.

8. The pad should exert slightly more pressure on the back side (hinge rod side) than on the front (outside).

9. If the back side of the pad touches only slightly or not at all, repeat the above procedure. Each time add paper washers under the pad until the desired pressure is obtained.

10. Wet the pad with a pad slick and remove wrinkles from the skin.

11. Place pad clamp(s) over the key(s) (Figure 36) and allow to dry for several hours, preferably overnight.

12. Remove clamp(s) and test the pad with a feeler.

13. If extra shims should be necessary after drying, mark the pad's location in the cup (Figure 37), add shim(s), and replace the pad in its original position.

14. Repeat any of the previous steps that may be necessary to obtain a smooth, well-seated pad.

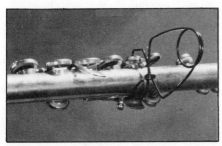

Figure 36. *Applying the pad clamp*

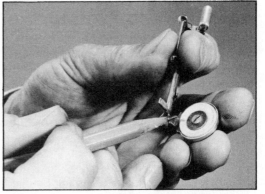

Figure 37. *Marking the pad's position*

Flute Repad

(List D Tools and Supplies)

Although a good, complete flute **repad** demands much time and skill, the following procedure is given for the director who wishes to pursue repairs to this point:

1. Remove all keys in the following order and place the screws in the mounting board (Figures 114 and 115, pages 190 and 191):
    a) Thumb key
    b) Upper C hinge rod
    c) D pivot screw
    d) All main line keys
    e) G hinge rod and key (two pad cups)
    f) Trill key pivot screws and keys
    g) G♯ hinge rod and keys

2. Remove the old pads and replace with new ones as described in the previous section.

3. Remove the corks from forked B♭ (or loosen the adjusting screw), and low C♯ **bridge** arms.

4. "Back off" the bridge **adjusting screws** on D, E, F, and A (Figure 38).

5. Replace the keys on the flute one at a time and adjust each one for proper seating before installing the next, in the following order:
    a) G♯
    b) Trill keys (glued pads)
    c) G keys
    d) C (glued pad)
    e) F♯ , F, E, and D (lower stack)
    f) A and B♭
    g) Low C
    h) Low C♯
    i) Low D♯

6. Follow standard pad clamping procedures.

7. After all pads have been seated properly, adjust the bridge keys as described on pages 79 and 80, Specific Woodwind Problems—Flute, Piccolo, Adjusting Bridge Keys, and recork the forked B♭ and low C bridge arms.

8. Check the cup opening with the key opening tool. (Remove or add cork to the key foot as needed.)

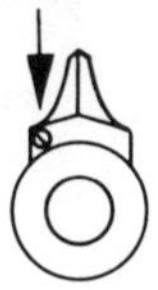

ADJUSTING
SCREW

Figure 38. *Adjusting the bridge screw*

Piccolo Padding

The piccolo repad represents one of the most difficult of all repair problems. It is not advisable for the band director to undertake this task himself. As in dent work or soldering, he should seek the advice of a local repairman if he considers it necessary to learn the skills needed for piccolo repadding.

Loose pads should be replaced in the following manner:

1. Replace the pad as near as possible in its original position.

2. Reglue it with liquid shellac (tube) or,

3. Heat the pad cup with a small-tipped soldering iron.

NOTE: Use of the bunsen burner on piccolo pads is apt to loosen and unseat the adjacent pads.

Except for other minor adjustments listed in Chapter 5, piccolo repairs should be handled only by a competent repairman.

Corking Tenons

(List B Tools and Supplies)

1. *Method A.* This is the simplest and can be used satisfactorily on all tenons.
    a) Remove protruding keys.
    b) Remove the old tenon cork and the shellac with the hooked and straight scrapers.
    c) Measure the width of the tenon groove and mark the cork. (The grain of the cork should be parallel with the cut cork's length, as shown in Figure 39.)
    d) Lay a straightedge on the marks and cut the work with a bench knife or razor blade. (Cut the cork approximately one inch longer than needed.)

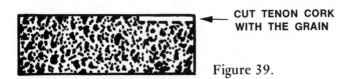

CUT TENON CORK
WITH THE GRAIN

Figure 39.

e) Test the cork's size by placing it in the tenon groove.
f) Bevel one end of the cut cork, as shown in Figure 40.
g) Coat the cleaned tenon groove, the bottom side of the cut cork, and its beveled end with a thin layer of contact cement (see Figure 40).

BEVEL

APPLY CONTACT
CEMENT HERE

Figure 40.
Beveling the tenon cork

h) Allow the cement to dry until it is no longer "tacky."
i) Press the beveled end of the cork into the tenon groove.
j) Starting at the beveled end, press the cut cork firmly into the groove until it overlaps and makes a tight contact with the bevel.
k) Cut away the excess cork with a bench knife or razor blade.
l) Bevel the edges of the cork (Figure 41) with a file or sanding stick.

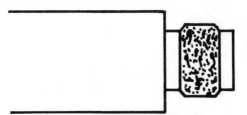

Figure 41.
Beveled tenon cork

m) Test the tenon for proper fit in its relative socket.
n) If the joint is too tight, cradle it in the left hand (right-handed person), palm up, with the left thumb on the tenon cork.
o) Insert a strip of garnet paper under the thumb and pull away briskly, simultaneously rotating the clarinet to the left to "sand off" the excess cork (Figure 42).

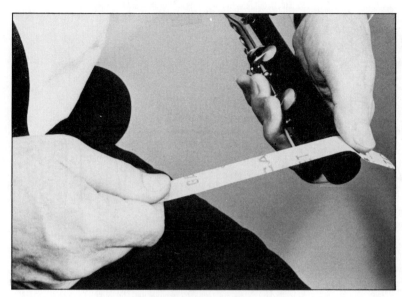

Figure 42.
*Sanding the
tenon cork*

p) Repeat until the excess cork has been removed evenly around the tenon.

q) When a proper fit is obtained, grease the cork.

2. *Method B.* Although not necessarily better, this method is preferred by many repairmen because it is much faster. It should, however, be used only on the small wood tenons (soprano clarinets and oboes), since shellac does not hold satisfactorily on many hard plastic instruments and on the large woodwind tenons.

a) Follow steps (a) through (f) of Method A.

b) Heat the stick shellac over the flame until it begins to melt.

c) Apply immediately to the cleaned tenon.

d) Repeat steps (b) and (c) until there is ample shellac to cover the tenon groove.

e) Heat the shellac spatula and smooth the shellac until there is equal distribution in the tenon groove.

f) Cradling the joint in the left hand as in (n) above, melt the shellac in the groove with the heated spatula and immediately press the cork into the groove, beveled end first, with the thumb (Figure 43).

g) Continue until the cork is installed in the groove (Figure 44).

h) Make sure that enough shellac coats the bevel so that a firm union is made with the overlapping cork.

i) With a bench knife, scraper, or screwdriver, "flake away" the excess shellac.

j) Follow steps (k) through (q) in Method A.

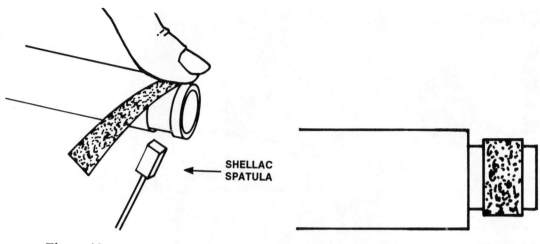

Figure 43.
Installing the cork with shellac

Figure 44.
Tenon cork before beveling

Cleaning Fish Skin Pads

(List A Supplies)

Sticking **fish skin pads** are most often caused by moisture accumulation on the pad skin. This is especially true when the player has consumed food or beverage containing sugar.

   To clean, slip a piece of eyeglass cleaning paper over the tone hole, depress the pad lightly, and pull the paper out slowly. Repeat the procedure until the pad is clean. For more stubborn accumulations, use a cloth saturated with alcohol.

Rebending Keys

(List A Tools)

Straightening bent keys involves a certain amount of risk, but the director should not hesitate if the bent key is functioning improperly.

   Using the flat nose pliers, bend the key to the correct position (Figure 94, page 128). If a pad cup has been bent, use whatever tools are necessary to bend the cup, but avoid damaging the tone hole and pad. Check the pad seating with the feeler.

Replacing Flat Springs

(List A Tools and C Supplies)

1. Remove the key from the instrument.

2. Select a spring of the proper size and strength.

3. Unscrew the spring screws from the key and install the new spring.

NOTE: On some saxophone models, the springs and screws are over-sized, making it impossible to install standard flat springs. These models should be sent to a repairman.

Replacing Needle Springs

(List D Tools and Supplies)

1. If a spring has been broken off even with the post, use the *broken* spring removing pliers (Figure 45).

2. To remove a whole, but weak, spring, use the *whole* spring removing pliers (Figure 46).

Figure 45. *Removing a broken spring*

Figure 46. *Removing a whole spring*

3. Select the correct size spring by testing it in the hole.

4. Using the jeweler's anvil and the small end of the dent hammer,

flatten the large end (flatten either end of a flute or piccolo *wire* spring).

CAUTION! A needle spring held between two fingers while flattening might result in a punctured finger. Holding the needle spring with a pair of common slip-joint pliers is the safest means of preventing a dangerous ricochet.

5. Insert in the post (about 1/16 inch of the flattened end should remain outside the post).

6. Using diagonal cutters (Figure 47), force the flattened end until it is even with the post.

7. Bend the spring so that it gives the proper key response.

NOTE: Threaded springs are standard equipment on some brands of saxophones. Unless the director wishes to invest in a complete set of these springs, he should send the instrument to a repair shop.

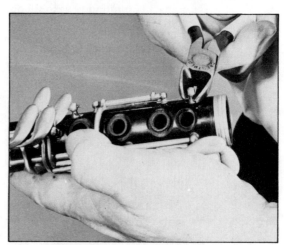

Figure 47.
Installing the needle spring

Removing Small Chips from Tone Holes (nonmetal)

(List B Tools)

1. Remove the key from the instrument.

2. With the correct size tone hole reamer held between the first two fingers and thumb, *very lightly* twist the reamer to the right until

the small chipped areas have been removed. Although this will somewhat alter the size and shape of the tone hole rim, it will allow a much better pad coverage.

Repairing Large Chipped Areas in the Tone Holes (nonmetal)

(List E Supplies)

1. Remove the key.

2. Clean the chipped area with alcohol.

3. Insert a tightly rolled piece of paper in the tone hole and let it unwind until it is against the inside of the tone hole walls (Figure 48).

Figure 48.
Preparation for tone hole patching

4. Mix a small amount of ebony compound as per directions.

5. With a small-bladed instrument, fill the cracked area and smooth out.

6. Allow twenty-four hours for drying.

7. Smooth the tone hole area with a flat file or tone-hole reamer (depending on the type of tone hole).

8. Replace the key or ring, and test the pad for coverage or clearance.

NOTE: When chipped or uneven areas appear in metal tone holes and cannot be straightened with round nose pliers or releveled with the tone hole file, the instrument should be sent to a repairman, as it will probably be necessary to solder a thin strip of metal to the tone hole wall.

Retightening Loose Tenon Rings

(List A Tools and Supplies)

If possible, this repair should be sent to a shop that has the proper ring-shrinking equipment. However, the following method, or similar methods, are acceptable substitutes:

1. Remove the ring and remember which edge will be replaced first (one end is sometimes wider).

2. Cut a narrow strip of waterproof paper to the ring groove's circumference.

3. Place the paper on the groove with the rough side against the wood.

4. Slip the ring over the paper (Figure 49). If extremely tight, tear 1/2 inch or so off the paper.

5. Tap the ring with the rawhide mallet until it is a distance of 1/16 inch from the groove shoulder.

6. Cut away the paper that is showing in the groove (Figure 49).

7. Tap the ring all the way against the shoulder.

8. Trim the remaining paper off the outside edge.

NOTE: The large ring on the rim of the woodwind bell requires a shrinking die and cannot be properly tightened otherwise.

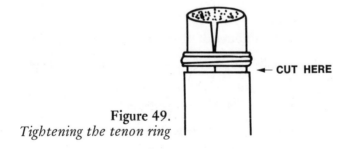

Figure 49.
Tightening the tenon ring

Recorking Thumb Rests

(List A Tools and Supplies)

1. Remove the old cork and clean the surface.

2. Heat the thumb rest.

3. Apply a piece of 1/32″ treated cork.

4. Trim the excess cork.

5. Smooth with a sanding stick or garnet paper.

Loose Screws

Loose screws may be tightened or replaced with List A tools and supplies.

Repairing Stripped Threads

(List E Supplies)

1. Remove the thumb rest or lyre socket.

2. Clean the screw holes with alcohol.

3. Mix a small amount of ebony compound and force it into the stripped hole.

4. Replace the thumb rest or lyre socket.

5. *Push* the screw into the soft compound.

6. Let it dry for twenty-four hours.

Repairing Stripped Strap Rings

(List E Supplies)

Follow the same procedure as in Stripped Threads.

Tightening Loose Posts (except metal woodwinds)

1. *Method A* (List A Tools and B Supplies)
    a) Remove the key(s).
    b) Remove the needle spring (Figure 46).
    c) Unscrew the post until it is halfway out of the body.

    d) Spread a small amount of powdered pumice around the screw
       (Figure 50).
    e) Retighten the post.
    f) If the post is not solid, follow Method B.

2. *Method B* (List A Tools and C Supplies)
    a) Follow steps (a) and (b) of Method A.
    b) Unscrew the post from the body.
    c) Slip one post shim over the threaded end of the post (Figure
       51).

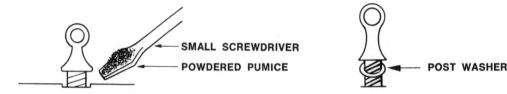

Figure 50. *Applying powdered*
pumice to the loose post
                                         Figure 51. *Post washer*

    d) Replace the post.
    e) If the post is still loose, follow Method C.

3. *Method C* (List A Tools and E Supplies)
    a) Follow steps (a) and (b) of Method B.
    b) Thoroughly clean the threaded sections on the screw and
       socket.
    c) Mix enough of the ebony compound to fill any cracks or
       chipped-off areas around the post.
    d) Fill the threaded hole and *push* while screwing the post into the
       hole.
    e) Remove or smooth the excess compound.
    f) Replace the key so that the post will be properly aligned.
    g) Use a flute pad clamp (or a rubber band for a large bore instru-
       ment) to hold the key in place while drying (twenty-four
       hours).
    h) Remove the key and replace the spring and key.

Occasionally a post will be so badly stripped that it will require a threaded
post bushing or an inlaid piece of wood in the damaged area. In such a case, refer
the job to a professional repairman.

Removing Loose Action in Pivot Screws (all woodwinds)

(List E Tools)

Constant use of a woodwind instrument eventually will cause loose action on pivot screw keys. The following procedure will remedy most of these problems:

1. Remove the pivot screw.

2. Select the correct size of countersinking (post) reamer.

3. Insert the reamer in the pivot screw socket (Figure 52).

4. Twist to the right one-half turn, removing only a *small amount* of metal.

5. Test the pivot screw and key for tightness.

6. Repeat as necessary, *removing only a small amount of metal* each time.

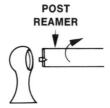

Figure 52. *Post reamer*

Relieving Pivot Screw Pressure

(List E Tools)

If the pivot screw has been countersunk too far, the key will bind when the pivot screw is inserted properly. The pressure can be relieved as follows:

1. Remove the pivot screw and key.

2. Using the proper size pivot screw reamer, remove a *small* amount of metal from the tapered hole in the key rod end (Figure 53).

3. Replace the key and test for free action.

4. Repeat as needed.

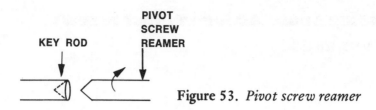

Figure 53. *Pivot screw reamer*

Relieving Hinge Tube Pressure

(List E Tools)

If pressure exists between the end of the hinge tubing and the post, thereby causing slow action, follow this procedure:

1. Follow procedures (3) and (4) in the following section (Eliminating Sluggish Key Action) before proceeding with step 2.

2. Remove the hinge rod and key.

3. Using the hinge tube shortener (Figure 54), remove a *small* amount of metal from the end of the tubing.

4. Replace the key and hinge rod, and test.

5. Repeat as needed.

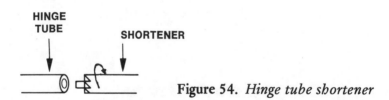

Figure 54. *Hinge tube shortener*

Eliminating Sluggish Key Action

(List A Tools and Supplies)

1. Check for loose or weak springs. If the spring is weak, bend it to the correct tension. (For installing new springs, see General Woodwind Procedures—Replacing Flat and Needle Springs, page 65.)

2. Check for dirty or rusted pivot screws and hinge rods.
   a) Unscrew the pivot screw or hinge rod one-fourth of a turn and test the key.

b) If the key now operates freely, place a drop of oil on the contact points.

c) Retighten the screw and test for freedom.

d) If the key is still sluggish, unscrew the pivot screw, clean with a pipe cleaner, reoil, and tighten. If the key operates by a hinge rod (rather than by a pivot screw), remove it completely from the key, insert an alcohol-saturated pipe cleaner through the hinge tube, clean the hinge rod, oil, and replace.

e) If the key is not yet "free," proceed to the next test.

3. Check for a twisted post (wooden or plastic instruments).

a) Visually check the post's alignment with the key.

b) If unable to detect a misalignment visually, use the flatnosed pliers in a slight twisting motion on the post while operating the key. If this procedure reveals the problem, follow the Loose Post procedures for wooden or plastic instruments (pages 69-70).

4. Check for bent posts (*metal instruments only*).

a) If the post is bent, take a small block of wood or a wooden dowel and place it against the inside (key side) of the post.

b) Using the rawhide mallet, tap *very lightly* against the post until the key operates freely.

CAUTION: Do not use this procedure on wooden or plastic instruments, as permanent damage can occur to the delicate threads in the body.

5. Check for binding tone hole rings.

If one of the rings is rubbing against the side of the tone hole, bend the ring with the flatnosed pliers.

CAUTION: Do not use a screwdriver with a prying motion against the tone hole wall. A broken tone hole will usually result.

6. Check for bridge arm binding.

a) Operate the sluggish key and inspect all moving parts.

b) Bridge arms often bind against a post or against their relative bridge key.

c) Bend the key arm slightly away from the obstruction.

7. Check for friction between the key (or its parts) and a loose pivot screw or hinge rod on an adjacent post.

NOTE: If the above seven procedures have not solved the problem, the instrument should be sent to a repair shop. The problem is obviously a bent body, a bent hinge rod, a bent hinge tube, or, on the flute, an accumulation of rust and grime inside the pinned hinge rod.

Removing Frozen Screws

(List D Tools)

1. Saturate the pivot screw or hinge rod areas with penetrating oil.

2. Let it set overnight.

3. If the screw slot has been "wallowed out," saw a new (or deeper) slot in the pivot screw or hinge rod with the jeweler's saw (Figure 55). Although this may mean sawing slightly into the post, it will not ruin the post.

4. Exert heavy pressure and try to unscrew.

CAUTION: Do not exert pressure with the screwdriver toward the body or toward the hand that holds the instrument. A "slipped" screwdriver can do serious damage to human flesh and muscle. Hold the instrument so that the screwdriver will hit the work table if it should slip (Figure 56).

5. Take the instrument to a repairman if the above procedure does not work.

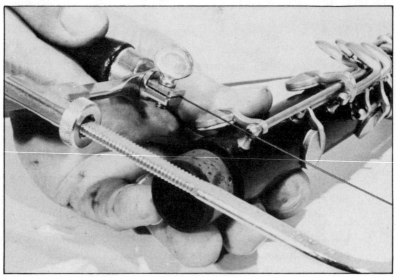

Figure 55. *Sawing a new slot*

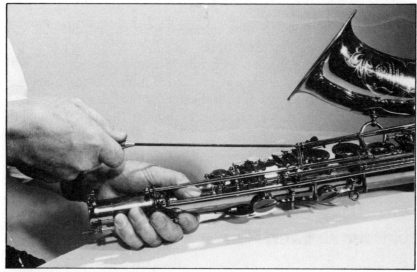

Figure 56. *Removing a frozen screw*

Repairing Worn Tenons

If a woodwind joint still wobbles after corking with extra thick cork, or if the tenon is chipped or cracked, the instrument should be sent to a repairman who is equipped to install tenon caps.

Removing Objects from "Stopped Up" Woodwinds (Flute and Trombone Cleaning Rods)

A broken swab, a pad, a ligature, a mouthpiece cap, or a can of cork grease often may become lodged inside the bore. Usually these objects can be removed without trouble.

1. Oboe and soprano clarinet
   a) Insert a flute rod into the small end of the bore.
   b) Be careful not to damage the thumb or octave tube. Push firmly toward the large end of the bore.
   c) If firm pressure does not remove the object, *send the instrument to a repair shop!*

2. Large clarinets and bassoon
   Use the trombone cleaning rod and repeat the steps listed in Number 1.

3. Saxophones
    a) Use the trombone cleaning rod and push the object toward the large end of the bore.
    b) If the object is a ligature that cannot be removed with a trombone cleaning rod, try jarring it loose by bumping the bell bow at the bottom with the heel of the hand.
    c) If neither method works, remove the key(s) near the lodged object and loosen it by reaching through a tone hole.

NOTE: Do not attempt any other method. Permanent damage to the bore, octave tube, or tone holes may result!

Repairing Broken Plastic Bodies

Many repair shops now have special cement that will mend any broken plastic instrument to complete satisfaction.

Refacing Mouthpieces

The need for a periodic inspection (at least once a year) of mouthpieces is often overlooked in clarinet and saxophone repairs. Even new mouthpieces will sometimes have warped rails, which prevent good tone production. Players often complain that they can only find one or two good reeds in each box, when in reality, the "good" reeds just happen to be warped in the same direction as the mouthpiece rails.

Most repair shops have repairmen (or access to specialists) who can accurately reface a mouthpiece to any specification. During a slack season, every director should have a skilled mouthpiece repairman visit his band classes to check all clarinet and saxophone mouthpieces, and to reface those that are chipped or warped. An expert can service the entire clarinet and saxophone sections in one class period by taking one or two students at a time. The rehearsal can continue without serious interruptions.

Removing Chalky Deposits from Mouthpieces

Under no circumstances should an attempt be made to *scrape* away these deposits. A repairman has the proper chemicals to remove them without damaging the mouthpiece.

NOTE: The following instructions are given for directors and instrumentalists who wish to "set-up" a pickle operation. However, special caution should be observed in mixing, using, and storing the solution, as skin burns, holes in clothing, lung damage (from inhalation of acid fumes), and rusted tools can result from careless use.

The soap solution should be replaced after cleaning five or six mouthpieces, as it becomes weak and ineffective. The pickle solution can be used to clean fifty or more mouthpieces. Dirty pickle solutions should be disposed of by emptying out of doors in useless soil that will not endanger greenery or animals.

(Two-quart, glass, kitchen canister with a wide mouth glass top; one gallon of muriatic acid; a container with a strong, soapy water solution; metal tongs; a mouthpiece brush; clean cloths or towels)

1. Fill the canister half full (one quart) of clear water.

2. Add one quart of muriatic acid. (Do not inhale fumes or splash on skin or clothing.)

3. Stir with tongs.

4. Using the tongs, pick up the mouthpiece and place slowly into the acid solution.

5. Place the cover on the canister and let the mouthpiece soak for five or ten minutes.

6. Using the tongs, lift the mouthpiece out of the canister and place immediately into a soapy solution.

7. Replace the lid on the canister.

8. Clean the loosened deposits with the mouthpiece brush.

9. Rinse the mouthpiece, tongs, and brush in clear water.

10. Dry the items with cloths or towels.

SPECIFIC WOODWIND PROBLEMS

Flute—Piccolo

Replacing Head Corks

(List A Tools and C Supplies)

1. Remove the crown.

2. Push the cork out the opposite (tenon) end (Figure 57).

3. Remove the threaded disc from the screw end.

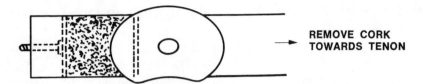

REMOVE CORK
TOWARDS TENON

Figure 57. *Removing flute tuning cork*

4. Remove the cork from the screw and save the cork for making trill key corks, key wedges, etc.

5. Clean the glue from the metal discs and from the screw.

6. Heat the disc that is permanently attached to the screw and coat the inside with white pad glue.

7. Immediately screw or push the new cork against the melted glue and hold until it cools.

8. Screw the threaded disc part way on, heat, and apply glue to its inside.

9. Immediately screw the disc up tight against the cork and hold until it cools.

10. Clean off any excess glue and grease the cork.

11. Using a tuning rod or wooden dowel rod, insert the cork (thread first) into the tenon end.

12. Push the cork into the joint until the ring on the **tuning rod** is in the center of the blow hole. (See Figure 26, page 28.)

13. Test for leakage (Flute, Physical Inspection, No. 4, page 29) after replacing the crown.

Loose Foot Tenons

(List C Tools)

1. Place the base of the can opener type tenon expander in the vise.

2. Insert the tenon between the two rollers (Figure 58).

3. Tighten the roller screw *lightly.*

4. Rotate the crank until the flute has made one complete revolution.

5. Move the tenon to a new position on the rollers and repeat.

Figure 58.
Expanding the foot tenon

6. Remove the flute and test the tenon with the foot joint.

7. Repeat the above procedure, *gradually* increasing roller tension until a desired fit is obtained.

Adjusting Bridge Keys

(List B Tools and Supplies)

1. Thumb $B^\flat$ (This problem is usually caused by a worn or missing cork on the small bridge arm.)
   a) Determine the needed cork thickness by inserting various thicknesses of cork between the thumb key foot and the bridge arm.
   b) Remove the A, $B^\flat$, and C keys and follow standard Key Corking procedures.

2. Forked $B^\flat$
   a) If the problem is missing or worn cork on the bridge arm, follow the key removal and adjusting procedures as listed in Repad, pages 60-61, and standard Key Corking procedures.
   b) If the problem is a bent bridge arm or in the $B^\flat$ adjusting screw, follow these procedures:
      (1) "Back off" the bridge adjusting screw on the F key (Figure 38, page 61, or Figure 106, page 187).
      (2) Using the flatnose pliers, bend the forked $B^\flat$ arm (standard) or adjust the screw to $B^\flat$ (new style) until equal feeler pressure is obtained between the F and $B^\flat$ pads.
      (3) Retighten the F bridge adjusting screw until equal feeler pressure exists on all three pads (F, $F^\sharp$, and $B^\flat$).

3. Second and third finger $F^\sharp$
   a) Loosen the third finger (D) bridge adjusting screw.
   b) Adjust the second finger (E) screw until equal pressure is obtained between the E and $F^\sharp$ pads.

    c) Repeat the procedure to obtain equal pressure on the D and F$\sharp$ pads.

4. Low C and C$\sharp$
    a) If the cork is missing on the C$\sharp$ bridge arm, remove the keys and recork.
    b) If the C$\sharp$ bridge arm is bent, rebend the arm (Figure 96, page 130) until equal pressure exists between C and C$\sharp$ when depressing the C key roller.

Removing Loose Action from the Keys

(List A Tools and Supplies)

1. For loose action caused by missing foot cork (the foot or arm that touches the body when the key is open), follow standard corking procedures.

2. If the cork is intact, the loose action may be removed by gluing (with liquid shellac) a small square(s) of paper on the foot cork.

3. Although the key feet may be bent to remove the loose action, this technique requires much practice.

Removing "Clicking" from Keys

(List A Tools)

If the keys have been properly corked, the only remaining key noise is likely to be caused by the trill B$\flat$ arm (above the F$\sharp$ key) when fingering A, G, or G$\sharp$. Using the flatnosed pliers, bend the arm up slightly. If a slight bending does not eliminate the contact, the right-hand key cups are opening too far and should have thicker foot corks.

Tightening the Head Joint Tenon

(List C Tools)

1. Tighten the flute head joint expander screw until the expander requires heavy, hand force to insert in the tenon end (Figure 59).

2. Make two or three turns.

Figure 59.
Expanding the head tenon

3. Test the tenon for size in the socket and repeat the above procedures, tightening the expander screw 1/16 turn each time until a snug fit is obtained.

Removing Head and Body Dents

(List E Tools)

1. Head joint dents
   a) Remove the tuning cork as described in Replacing Head Corks, page 78 (Figure 57).
   b) Clamp the base of the head joint mandrel in the vise.
   c) Slip the head joint on the mandrel, tenon end first.
   d) Use the tip of the mandrel to push out the dents or use the dent hammer as needed.

2. Body dents
   a) Remove all keys as described in General Woodwind Procedures, Flute Repad, pages 60-61.
   b) Clamp the base of the body mandrel in the vise.
   c) Slip the body over the mandrel.
   d) *Being careful to avoid tone hole damage,* remove the dents by pushing against the mandrel tip or by using a dent hammer as needed.

Oboe—English Horn

Due to the intricate construction of the oboe and English horn, the director should restrict his involvement with them to care and maintenance, testing, and the simplest of repair problems. The flat and needle spring assortments, for instance, are not likely to have more than one or two sizes (or strengths) that are correct for the oboe. The pads are made of both skin and cork and are of special thicknesses, many keys must be replaced simultaneously, etc.

If, however, the director wishes to attempt repairs, the following procedure is standard for the removal of the keys on most oboes.

Disassembling

(List D Tools and Supplies)

> *NOTE:* Figures 116, 117, and 118 (Appendix) will be helpful. On many oboes and professional clarinets, pivot screws have been fitted to a specific post or key and should be kept separated.

1. Remove the side B♭ key from the upper joint.

2. Remove the G♯ pivot screw.

3. Remove the hinge rod from the main line or stack.

4. Unhook all springs from their **spring blocks** and remove the keys. Be careful to place the screws and hinge rods in the mounting board and arrange the keys in their proper order.

5. Remove the two octave "teeter" keys (usually mounted with one hinge rod).

6. Remove the lower octave key.

7. Remove the upper trill key lever.

8. Remove the lower trill key lever.

9. Remove the two trill keys (one hinge rod).

10. Remove the left-hand G♯ lever.

11. Remove the thumb lever.

12. On the lower joint, remove the hinge rod from the bottom of the long, low B♭ lever tubing.

13. Remove the pivot screw from the post under the B♭ spatula.

14. Carefully remove the entire B♭ tubing mechanism from the body and from its linkage with other keys.

15. Remove the D♯ key.

16. Remove the forked F key.

17. Remove the B hinge rod (on the lower post).

18. Remove the pivot screw from the upper post on the B key.

19. Remove the pivot screw from the lower post of C.

20. Carefully remove the B, C, and C♯ keys.

21. Remove the trill key **teeter**.

22. Remove the hinge rod from the stack keys.

23. Unhook the springs and remove the keys.

24. Remove the F♯ trill key.

From this point, the director can perform most major repairs for which he has equipment. But it is advised that no attempts be made at replacing cork pads, since they seldom deteriorate and are difficult to seat properly.

Leaking skin pads can now be replaced and seated individually with a minimum of interference from adjacent keys. Other problems (loose posts, broken springs, joint corks, etc.) should also be corrected while the instrument is disassembled.

Bridge keys may be adjusted with the adjusting screws, by recorking, or by bending as described in previous sections.

NOTE: If a repair kit does not contain oboe pads, clarinet pads may be used as follows:

1. Select a clarinet pad about two sizes smaller than the oboe pad cup.

2. Puncture the pad.

3. Flatten the pad between the smooth jaws of the flatnose pliers.

Assembling

To assemble, reverse the above procedures. *Use caution to prevent bending the hinge rods and tubings.*

Soprano Clarinets

Disassembling

(List A Tools)

> *NOTE:* See Figures 114 and 119 (pages 190 and 193). Also see note on disassembling oboe.

1. Remove the register key (upper joint).
2. Unscrew all side key hinge rods.
3. Remove the four side keys simultaneously.
4. Remove the thumb ring.
5. Remove the $A^\flat$ key.
6. Remove the A key.
7. Remove the stack keys.
8. Remove the $C^\sharp$ -$G^\sharp$ key.
9. Remove the $E^\flat$ -$B^\flat$ trill key.
10. Remove the left-hand levers (lower joint).
11. Remove the low F and $G^\sharp$ hinge rod and keys.
12. Remove the low E key.
13. Remove the low $F^\sharp$ key.
14. Remove the left-hand low F lever.
15. Remove the ring keys.
16. Remove the B-$F^\sharp$ trill key.

While disassembled, the clarinet should be thoroughly checked for such problems as loose posts, rusted or broken springs, chipped tone holes, uncorked keys, or poor pads. The hinge rods and tubes can also be cleaned and oiled.

Assembling

To assemble, reverse the above procedure. Oil all screws as they are inserted.

Installing Silencer Skins in Lever Keys

(List A Tools and Supplies)

1. Remove the left-hand lever keys.
2. Wet the silencer skins and place them over the lever pivots.
3. Push into the arm holes.
4. If there is still too much loose action, add extra skins.

Adjusting the A and A♭ Keys

Although some brands of clarinets have a flat area for cork on top of the A key, the cork will wear away so rapidly that it is futile to try to keep it corked. If the adjusting screw is set properly, there should be a minimum of noise without the cork. Use the feeler and adjust the screw accordingly.

Adjusting the Thumb Ring

(List A Tools and Supplies)

1. Check the thumb ring for level closing with the thumb tone hole while fingering F.
2. If the cork is missing or worn on the foot of the thumb ring or on the F key arm, recork as needed.
3. If the corks are intact but the thumb ring is out of adjustment with the F, bend the F arm up or down as needed. (This should be done *only* if the arm and foot are corked correctly.)

Adjusting the Key Rings

(List A Tools)

1. If the pads are of proper thickness, the key rings, when depressed, should be level with the tops of their respective tone holes.
2. Insert the pad slick between the ring and the tone hole, or between the pad and the tone hole (for bending).

3. If the pad closes first, place the pad slick under it. Reverse the procedure if the ring closes first.

4. Press lightly on the ring to bend it.

5. Remove the pad slick.

6. The ring should now be even with the top of its tone hole when the pad is fully closed.

7. Repeat as needed.

CAUTION: The use of a screwdriver or other tool for the above procedure may result in punctured pads or in chipped tone holes.

Adjusting the Bridge Key

(List A Tools and Supplies)

The bent **bridge key** on the upper joint is a common problem. Not only will it prevent the use of the forked E♭-B♭, but it will often bind on the C♯-G♯ key.

1. Check the underside of the upper bridge key for proper corking.

2. Cork with a thin cork if necessary. Since the upper bridge key rests on the lower joint bridge key, it is unnecessary to cork that part of the upper bridge which touches the body.

3. Bend the bridge key to its proper position (Figure 101, page 138), insert the lower joint, and test the two pads for unison closings.

Adjusting the Low E and F Bridge

(List A Tools)

On most clarinets the low F presser foot (or crow foot) is rigid and rarely needs to be bent. Bend it if necessary, but if it shows *no* sign of being crooked, follow these procedures:

1. Test the two pads with a feeler for equal pressure.

2. If the low E is tighter, place the **pad slick** (or use pliers, as shown in Figure 102, page 138) under the low E pad and bend the E spatula down slightly.

3. Test, and repeat as necessary.

4. If the low F pad is tighter, hold the low E pad on its tone hole and lift its spatula lightly.

5. Repeat as necessary.

6. If there is loose action between the spatulas and the presser foot, press down on the spatula that is higher and bend the spatula arm (the arm that connects to the lever key) down as necessary.

7. For further information, see Chapter 5, Soprano Clarinets, item 2.

NOTE: Due to differences in the models and styles of various woodwind brands, the above woodwind repair procedures should be modified to fit the instrument. On some clarinets and saxophones, for instance, a **set screw** locks the pivot screw in position and must be unscrewed before removing the pivot screw. The director should check for the presence of other irregularities before beginning each repair.

Unsticking Tenons

(List A Tools and Supplies)

On new wooden clarinets, the **tenons** will often swell and stick due to the absorption of moisture from playing.

1. Allow the clarinet to dry at room temperature so that the tenon will return to its normal size. (Sometimes it will take several days.)

2. Remove the tenon from the socket.

NOTE: Most stuck tenons are caused by leaving the clarinet assembled after playing! If this is not the cause, proceed with step 3.

3. With a piece of garnet paper on the index finger, lightly sand the walls of the tenon socket.

4. Oil the bore and the socket with a good bore oil or olive oil, and allow overnight drying.

5. If the tenon persists in sticking, send it back to the dealer or to a competent repairman who has the necessary equipment for accurate reaming and lathe work.

NOTE: If a *real emergency* exists, the stuck tenon may be removed by inserting a knife blade or thin wedge between the joints and prying them apart. *Be careful to avoid denting the ring and wooden shoulder.*

Resetting the Octave (Register) Tube

(List D Tools and A Supplies)

If a leak has been found around the **register tube**, follow these procedures:

1. Remove the register key.

2. Place one hand over the register tube while holding the upper joint.

3. Insert a large screwdriver into the bore and push upward on the tube. This method works only on tapered and unthreaded tubes. Do *not* attempt to remove a threaded tube, such as the oboe tube, in this manner.

4. Clean the outside of the register tube with waterproof or garnet paper.

5. Place the tube, large end first, on an awl.

6. Heat the tube and coat it with stick shellac.

7. While the glue is still in liquid form, push the tube into the hole.

8. When the shellac cools, flake away the excess shellac.

9. On most clarinets, the tube will protrude about 1/16 inch above the body.

10. Replace the register key and test for leaks.

Alto and Bass Clarinets

Octave or Register Key Problems

(List A Tools and Supplies)

Register key mechanisms on bass and alto clarinets vary from a simple two-key arrangement on the upper joint to an intricate maze of bridge rods and keys extending from the neck register key to the third finger, right hand. Therefore it is impractical to describe and illustrate the techniques necessary for adjusting all models.

If the model is the vented pad (first finger, left hand) type, see Chapter 5, Most Frequent Problems, Alto and Bass clarinets, item 1-a.

If the model has an automatic register key mechanism, use the following points for determining the correct procedure for adjusting:

1. The lower register key should operate (usually) from third line B to fourth line D.

2. From fourth line E upward, the upper key (usually on the neck) should open and the lower key should close.

3. Recork or bend the bridge mechanisms as needed for proper operation.

One-Piece Body Construction

The one-piece body on bass and alto clarinets is most practical and should be seriously considered when purchasing new instruments. A good alternative is to have the existing two-piece models made into one-piece models by a repairman. Although this also means purchasing a new case, the money and time saved on repairs will justify the conversion.

Disassembling

(List A Tools)

Follow the procedure given for soprano clarinets, except:

1. Remove the third finger (left-hand) hinge rod and keys before removing $C^\sharp$-$G^\sharp$, and,

2. Remove the right-hand stack keys in accordance with their design.

NOTE: Use a clarinet mounting board (Figure 114 and Figure 119, pages 190 and 193) as a guide.

Adjusting the Bell Key

(List A Tools)

1. Check for correct corking.

2. Reseat the pad if needed.

3. Bend the key arm or the bridge arm under the low E spatula for unison closing with the low E and F keys.

Adjusting the Bridge Keys

(List A Tools and Supplies)

1. If the key felts are missing, install new ones with liquid shellac.

2. If the felt is intact, use the pad slick and bend the key arms for proper closings.

3. Test with a leak light.

4. If an individual pad is not seating properly, heat with the bunsen burner and adjust as described in Seating Glued Pads, pages 56-57 (except saxophones).

Bassoons

Though most problems of bassoon repair should be handled by a competent repairman, some can be managed by any director who has the time, skill, and patience. Figures 120 through 125, pages 194 through 197, may be valuable aids.

Recorking the End Bow

(List E Supplies)

On some plastic models the tube in the end bow is removable. If leaking is occurring there, use a thick lubricant to seal it. If a leak has been discovered on standard models (by means of water stains or smoke leakage) around the flange on the end bow, follow these procedures:

1. Remove the bow cap.

2. Mark the end bow so that it may be replaced correctly.

3. Remove the two screws and the end bow, *taking care not to destroy the gasket.*

4. Using the old gasket for a pattern, make a new slightly oversized gasket from the sheet of 3/32″ cork.

5. Thoroughly clean the end bow flange and its corresponding surface on the joint, so that no grease or glue remains.

NOTE: From this point, repair practices differ. Although use of the following method will mean that replacement of the gasket will be necessary whenever the end bow is removed later, it offers a sure and safe way of sealing the end bow.

6. Coat the end bow flange, its corresponding surface on the joint, and *both* sides of the cork with contact cement.

7. After an ample drying time, place the cork on the end bow flange and press the cork against the flange thoroughly, so that the entire surface will adhere. Use a *clean* tool or wooden dowel rod end for pressing, so that no foreign matter will be left on the outer coated side of the cork.

8. Trim away the excess cork from the tubing and from the outside flange.

9. Observe the alignment marks (Step 2) and place the end bow on the joint.

10. With a wooden dowel or a screwdriver handle, press the flange firmly against the joint.

11. Replace the holding screws.

12. Test for leaks.

If a hole is found in the tubing bow, or a leak around the metal collar that attaches to the wooden body, send the bassoon to the repair shop.

Repairing Stripped Threads

(List A Tools and E Supplies)

1. If the stripped threads are in the wooden body, install an oversized screw or follow the procedure for Stripped Threads in the General Woodwind Procedures section, page 69.

2. If the stripped threads are in a metal part, send the instrument to a repair shop that has the proper drills and **taps**.

Reseating the Pads

(List A Tools)

Due to the construction of the bassoon, many keys cannot be heated, bridge mechanisms adjusted, or pads tested for leaks without first removing a key guard or an adjacent key(s). After removing the obstructing devices, reseat the pads, adjust the bridge mechanisms, and test the keys for leakage as previously described in Physical Inspection, items 5 through 8, page 35.

Recorking the Bocal

Since the bocal cork is extremely close to the soldered nib, inexperienced attempts at heating the bocal for recorking could result in a loose and leaking nib. This process is best left to the experienced repairman.

Saxophones

Adjusting the Octave Mechanism

(List A Tools)

1. If the octave mechanism does not function as described in Chapter 2, Saxophone, Physical Inspection, item 4, page 37, check the octave bridge for damage (often caused by placing the instrument in the case without first inserting the end plug).

2. Bend the octave bridge or recork as needed (Figure 104, page 142).

3. If the bridge key has not been damaged and the upper octave key remains open, bend the key as shown in Figure 60.

4. If the upper octave does not open when fingering upper A, reverse the procedure in Number 3 above.

5. Test.

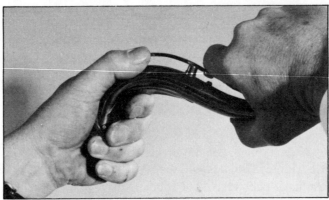

Figure 60. *Adjusting the upper octave key*

Expanding the Tenon

(List C Tools)

When the neckpipe is loose in the tenon socket after the neck screw has been tightened, follow these procedures:

1. Check the inside of the tenon for excess solder. If present, scrape it out before proceeding.

2. Place the base of the tenon expander in the vise.

3. Insert the tenon between the rollers (Figure 61).

4. Tighten the tension screw *lightly*.

5. Turn the crank until the neck has made one revolution.

6. Continue moving the tenon to a new position until the entire tenon has been pressed by the rollers.

7. Test the tenon for tightness in its socket.

8. Repeat as needed, *slightly* increasing the tension screw pressure each time.

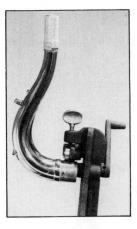

Figure 61.
Expanding the neck tenon

Installing Key Bumpers

(List A Tools and Supplies)

1. Clean the felt receiving area.

2. Select the correct sized **bumper** and cut, if necessary, to the length that will produce the proper key opening.

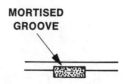

Figure 62. *Type A felt holder*

Figure 63. *Type B felt holder*

Figure 64. *Type C felt holder*

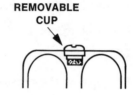

Figure 65. *Type D felt holder*

3. Place a small amount of liquid shellac on, or in, the felt receiver and install the felt.

4. On Type D cups, it will be more convenient to remove the cups from the **key guard** for felt installation.

5. On Type B felt receivers, spread the tabs, cut the felt for size, insert the felt (gluing is optional), and bend the tabs to hold the felt.

6. On Type A key guards, more lasting results will be obtained by using contact cement.

Disassembling

(List A Tools)

The following procedures must be modified, when necessary, for each brand and model. Remove the keys in the following order, using Figures 126, 127, and 128 (pages 198 and 199) as aids:

1. Neck octave key

2. Octave bridge

3. Thumb key and lower octave key

4. Palm keys

5. Side C

6. Side B♭

7. Low C and D$\sharp$

8. Upper stack keys

9. Upper E

10. Teeter key

11. G$\sharp$ lever

12. Low C$\sharp$

13. Bell keys (B, B$\flat$)

14. G$\sharp$ key

15. Lower stack keys

Disassembled, the saxophone can be scrubbed, tone holes can be leveled (D tools), keys can be corked, pads can be replaced, new springs installed, hinge rods and tubings cleaned and oiled, and individual pads seated without interference from adjacent pads.

To assemble the keys, reverse the above order. On some models, the needle spring must be inserted through a hole in the key arm instead of nesting in a spring block. In this case, insert the spring into the hole before securing the key with the hinge rod.

Installing Neck Corks

(List C Tools and Supplies)

1. Remove the old cork.

2. Sand the cork area clean.

3. Heat the neck and apply the stick shellac to the area to be corked. A thin layer should coat the entire area.

4. Let the shellac cool and place the cork on the neckpipe.

5. Wrap cotton cord around the cork (Figure 66).

6. Holding the cork protector over the neckpipe end, heat the neck-pipe bore with the bunsen burner (Figure 66) until the shellac is again melted. (The cork should twist easily on the neckpipe.)

7. Making sure the cork is in position, allow the shellac to cool.

8. Remove the cord.

9. Test the mouthpiece for correct cork size.

10. To remove excess cork, sand off as in tenon cork sanding (Figure 67) or as in a shoeshining motion (Figure 68).

11. The sides of finished cork should be *parallel* so that the mouthpiece will be snug when placed near the end. It will also enable the player to push the mouthpiece all the way up without cracking the mouthpiece. Only the saxophone with the tuning device needs to have a tapered cork.

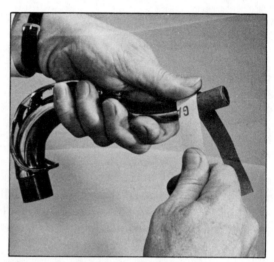

Figure 67. *Sanding the neck cork*

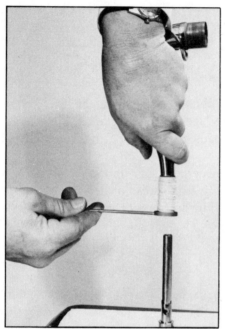

Figure 66. *Heating the neck cork*

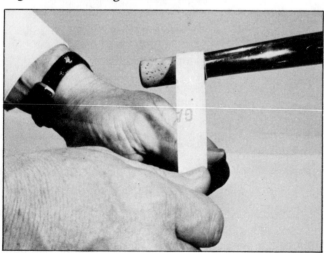

Figure 68.
*Sanding the neck cork
(optional)*

Leveling the Tone Holes

(List D Tools)

CAUTION: If the unlevel tone hole has been caused by a body dent, *do not file the tone hole until the body dent has been removed!*

1. Remove the key(s).

2. Place the file on the tone hole.

3. While holding the file flat on the tone hole with the thumb (Figure 69), move the file "tang" in a sidewise motion (Figure 70).

Figure 69. *Filing the tone hole*

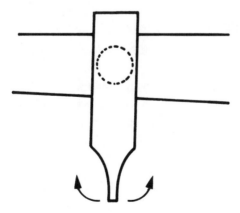

Figure 70. *Filing sidewise*

4. Continue the process until the tone hole is level, as evidenced by file marks on the entire tone hole rim.

5. Replace the key(s) and reseat the pad.

NOTE: Some tone holes are too small for the large tone hole file, and some posts prevent the use of the file in a sidewise motion. If that situation exists, use a narrower file in a back-and-forth motion, being careful to keep the file level (Figure 111, page 189).

Replacing Key Rollers

(List D Tools and E Supplies)

If the key roller screw cannot be loosened in the conventional manner (Removing Frozen Screws, page 74), follow this procedure:

1. Remove the key or lever from the saxophone.
2. Break the roller tubing with the slip-joint pliers.
3. Using the slip-joint pliers, remove the frozen screw rod.
4. Remove the rust and plier marks from the screw rod.
5. Measure and cut a new roller.
6. Drill the roller to the screw rod size.
7. Bevel the edges of the roller.
8. Oil the new roller and place it on the key.

Tuning Mechanism Leaks

(List A Supplies)

Some old style saxophones have tuning devices on the neckpipe. Although they are constructed to precision, the lubricant may dry or "break down" over a long period of time and allow minute leaks. If a smoke test reveals leaks in the tuning mechanism, follow these procedures:

1. Unscrew the mechanism from the neck.
2. Clean both parts with kerosene.
3. Apply a liberal coating of mutton tallow or good petroleum grease to the threads and tubing.

4. Replace the mechanism on the neck and remove the excess grease.

5. Test the neck for leaks.

Adjusting the Bridge Mechanisms

(List B Tools and Supplies)

If the bridge key cork is missing or worn, follow the standard key corking procedures (Corking Keys, page 54). Use the correct thickness of key cork. If recorking is unnecessary, follow these steps:

1. Upper B
    Bend the B foot up or down as needed to close both keys together.

2. Upper C
    a) Check for a missing key felt.
    b) Bend the C arm or the C foot as needed to make the three pads (A, B$^\flat$, C) close simultaneously.

3. G$^\sharp$
    On most saxophones the G$^\sharp$ lever spring is stronger than the G$^\sharp$ key spring and works with an opposite or "overriding" action. If the lever does not close the key properly,
    a) Increase the tension on the lever key spring, or,
    b) Install a thicker cork on the bridge arm.

4. F$^\sharp$ to G$^\sharp$ bridge arm
    a) On saxophones with bridge adjusting screws, adjust the screw for unison closings of the F, F$^\sharp$, and G$^\sharp$ keys.
    b) On others, bend the bridge arm or recork until the three pads close together.

5. Forked B$^\flat$
    a) Bend the B$^\flat$ bridge arm (under the F$^\sharp$ bridge arm) so that the F, F$^\sharp$, and upper B$^\flat$ close simultaneously.
    b) Hold the G$^\sharp$ lever down and check F, F$^\sharp$, G$^\sharp$, and upper B$^\flat$ for unison closings.

6. Second and third finger F$^\sharp$
    a) Check the second finger pad for unison closing with F$^\sharp$.
    b) Check the third finger pad in the same manner.
    c) Check the second and third finger pads as in step 5-b above.

NOTE: On some older model saxophones a D$^\sharp$ trill pad is operated by the second finger, right-hand key. Some repairmen will permanently close them to prevent maintenance problems. If this pad is allowed to remain in operation, it should be adjusted to close simultaneously with the E, F$^\sharp$, G$^\sharp$, and upper B$^\flat$ key pads.

7. Low C$^\sharp$
    a) One saxophones that have a bridge between low B and C$^\sharp$, finger low C$^\sharp$ and low B at the same time and check for unison closings.
    b) Adjust the bridge arm as needed.

8. Low B$^\flat$
    a) The low B$^\flat$ lever should also close the low B.
    b) If the two pads do not seat equally, recork (or felt) the table key bridge, or bend the table key bridge, or bend the bridge mechanism that is located on the key rod or on the key cup.

9. As a final check, finger low B$^\flat$ and check for leaks in the G$^\sharp$ key, since a leak in the G$^\sharp$ often prevents good resonance in the bell key notes.

Reseating Pads

See Seating Glued Pads (Saxophones), pages 57-58.

Repairing the Sticking G$^\sharp$ Pad

(List B Supplies)

The G$^\sharp$ pad on many saxophones often retains saliva or condensed breath moisture. Since the G$^\sharp$ key spring is weak, the pad will sometimes fail to open when fingering G$^\sharp$. One of two methods will probably eliminate this problem:

1. Clean the tone hole rim and the pad, and coat the pad with neatsfoot oil.

2. With a small cotton swab, apply a small amount of powdered pumice to the tone hole groove in the pad.

Silencing Special Keys

(List A Tools)

Some saxophones have special bridge arms and keys that cannot be corked conventionally. Figure 71 represents a typical bridge arm that fits into a fork or slot. For other styles of special arms, see Figure 129, page 200.

APPLY TAPE HERE

Figure 71. *The special arm*

1. Remove the lever from the saxophone.

2. Clean the prong.

3. Using plastic tape, wrap the prong until the correct thickness is obtained.

4. Remove the excess tape that protrudes beyond the prong end.

5. Test the prong in the fork or slot.

6. Replace the lever.

NOTE: Silencer tubing (**macaroni**) is available from manufacturers for these special levers, but it is impractical for the director to purchase it in quantities.

Special Pads

Several brands and models of saxophones require special pads designed to give maximum resonance and intonation. Some models require special techniques for replacement and should be sent to a competent repairman. Others can be ordered through a dealer and installed by the director. In either case, replacement pads should conform to the original style, and should be installed without alteration of the pad cup.

BRASSES

Piston Valve Instruments

Removing Stuck Mouthpieces

(List A Tools)

Stuck mouthpieces occur more often than any other single brass repair problem. Consequently, more damage is done to mouthpieces and mouthpipes by unorthodox removal techniques than by any other brass repair attempts.

Although stuck mouthpieces can sometimes be removed by using pliers or a rawhide mallet, broken braces, twisted neckpipes, scarred mouthpieces, and ovalled shanks are often the results of such attempts.

A good mouthpiece puller can be purchased for less than the cost of replacing a mouthpipe and *should be standard equipment in every school that has a band program.*

1.   Select the correct size collars.

2.   Place one collar in the bottom shoulder of the puller.

3.   Place the mouthpiece and the mouthpiece receiver in the puller (Figure 72).

4.   Place the second collar in the top shoulder of the puller.

5.   Twist both screws *simultaneously* until the mouthpiece is free.

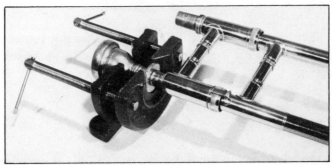

Figure 72. *Pulling a mouthpiece*

Refinishing Mouthpieces

Due to a variety of body chemicals, some individuals are allergic to brass. To prevent lip infections, the director should insist that all brass mouthpieces be replated when the plating has become worn or when the mouthpiece rim is dented or scarred. Since allergies sometimes include silver, having the mouthpiece replated with gold or nickel will often alleviate reactions.

Straightening Mouthpiece Shanks

(List B Tools)

1.   Insert one jaw of the roundnosed pliers into the shank (Figure 73).

2.   Alternately grip the handles and rotate the mouthpiece to remove the dents.

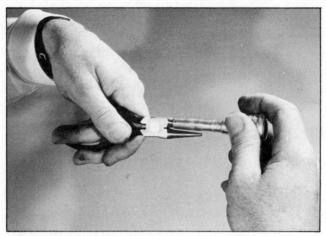

Figure 73. *Straightening the shank*

3. Light "taps" with the dent hammer (List C tools) will permit more accurate dent removal.

4. For larger mouthpieces, use a tapered punch and a dent hammer (Figure 105, page 146).

Replacing Water Key Corks

(List A Supplies)

Replacing water key corks is very simple and should be a standard procedure for the director or for a student repair assistant.

1. Remove the old cork and the glue.

2. Select a *good* cork.

3. Place a small amount of liquid shellac on the small end of the cork.

4. Insert the cork in the cup and force it into place.

5. Slice or sand the cork until it seats level on the **nipple**.

Replacing Water Key Springs

(List D Supplies)

1. Remove the slide if the water key is on a removable slide.

2. Unscrew the axle or hinge rod.

3. Remove the old spring.

4. Insert the new spring on or in the water key and replace it in the **saddle** or yoke.

5. Bend the spring ends around the yoke post.

6. Cut off the excess ends.

Pulling Stuck Slides

(List A Tools and Supplies)

1. Soak all areas (including the bore) of the stuck slide with penetrating oil.

2. Let it set overnight.

3. Try to remove the slide with finger pressure.

4. If it is a main tuning slide with a large **slide bow** and does not have a cross brace, *do not attempt further action if it remains stuck.* Send it to a repair shop!

5. If the slide has a cross brace on the slide tubing (do not confuse it with a cross brace on the sleeve), tap the brace lightly with the rawhide mallet on the side that is stuck (usually the bottom). Repeated *light* tapping will, in many cases, unstick the slide. If not, send it to a repair shop.

6. If the stuck slide is one that has a small slide bow (first, second, or third valve slides), insert a tapered rod (i.e., a jaw of the round-nosed pliers) against the inside of the bow, and tap with a rawhide mallet (Figure 74).

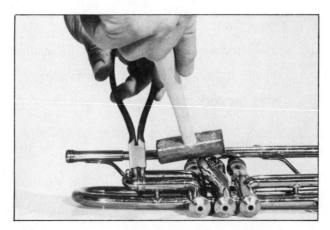

Figure 74. *Removing the stuck small slide*

CAUTION: Make sure that the tapered rod does not dent an adjacent tube, and that repeated tappings do not allow the instrument to slide off the holding mandrel onto the floor.

7. Small slides may also be removed by pulling on leather thongs, ropes, rags, and belts that have been inserted through the slide bow. But this often results in unsoldered joints, broken braces, and warped tubing. If the technique described in Number 6 above does not free the slide, send it to a repair shop.

8. For larger slides (baritone, flugelhorn, bass) use a tapered mandrel (drumstick, etc.) that fits snugly into the inner side of the slide bow, as in Figure 74.

9. After pulling, clean the corroded slides with fine, waterproof paper and the sleeves by swabbing. Regrease and insert the slides separately in a spiralling motion until each slide works freely.

Removing Frozen Valve Caps

(List A Tools)

1. With a rawhide mallet, tap the sides and end of the valve cap.

2. Try to unscrew.

3. Repeat as needed, tapping with a little more force.

4. If the frozen valve cap is a top cap, damage can be done to the bell or neckpipe unless care is used when striking the cap. To be safe, follow these procedures:
    a) Remove the bottom valve cap and the valve spring (if a bottom type).
    b) Remove the finger button.
    c) Holding the valve in the "down" position (Figure 75), tap down on the valve cap until it is loose.

Removing Stuck Tuning Bits (Sousaphones)

(List A Tools)

1. Remove the mouthpipe from the sousaphone.

2. Tap the bit **receiver** or **ferrule** with the rawhide mallet.

3. Repeat as needed.

Figure 75.
Loosening a top valve cap

Freeing Stuck or Sluggish Piston Valves

(List E Tools)

1. Do not force the valve from the casing.

2. Pull the tuning slide on the stuck valve.

3. Check for the presence of foreign matter (a pencil, a piece of a flexible swab, etc.) by looking through the open tubing into the valve casing.

4. Check for a bent tuning slide (often caused by forcing books, gym shorts, etc., into the case).
    a) If a bent slide is evident, grasp the instrument firmly by the valve casings.
    b) With the fingers, pull the tuning slide back to its original position.
    c) Check the valve.

5. If the valve cannot be pulled from its casing by grasping the finger button (after overnight soaking with penetrating oil), the instrument should be sent to a repair shop.

CAUTION: Do not try to "drive out" the stuck valve with a dowel or similar round object. The bottom end of the *hollow* valve is sealed with a thin brass washer that will be ruined by such action.

6. If the valve is still tight but can be removed with normal finger pressure, check for dents in the casing.
    a) Use a valve-cleaning rod and clean cloth to clean the casing.

b) Hold the casing up to the light and locate the casing dent (usually a "bright" spot).
c) Verify the dent by locating it on the outer case.
d) Send the large brasses to a repair shop.

NOTE: Procedures (e) through (m) following are for cornets and trumpets. Only the director with considerable repair experience should attempt this procedure.

e) Adjust the reamer to the casing size by operating its top and bottom adjusting nuts simultaneously.
f) Place the square end of the reamer in the vise.
g) Holding the instrument with both hands, place the bottom end of the valve casing over the reamer and rotate slowly clockwise, keeping equal pressure on both hands.
h) If the reamer was set to the exact size of the casing, it will remove only the dent and will not mar the remainder of the casing walls.
i) Continue the clockwise motion until the reamer blades are visible on the above upper casing opening.
j) Remove the instrument in a slow, clockwise motion, keeping equal pressure on both hands.
k) Hold the casing to the light.
l) There should now be a slightly larger bright spot at the dent location.
m) Check the valve for freedom.

7. Check for gummy or corroded deposits on the valve.
   a) Using a nonabrasive metal polish, clean and polish the valve with clean cloths.
   b) Wash the valve in soapy water to remove the polish residue.
   c) Clean the valve casing.
   d) Oil and test the valve.

8. Check for the presence of filmy deposits.
   a) Inspect the valve ports for the presence of a filmy buildup.
   b) Clean the valve and ports in soapy water.
   c) Clean the casing.
   d) Oil and replace the valve.
   e) If the valve is now free, clean the entire instrument to prevent a repetition of this problem.

9. Check for a binding valve guide.
   a) If the guide is one of the movable types, check for proper installation.

b) If the guide is attached to the piston wall, check it for burrs.

c) Unless the problem can be solved with minor efforts, send the instrument to a repair shop. Damage to pistons can be caused by incompetent attempts to remove or replace the fixed guide.

Aligning the Valve Ports

(List B Tools and A Supplies)

Most piston valve instruments have a line around the valve stem to indicate the correct open position. The line should be even with the top edge of the valve cap (Figure 76). The "down" valve position and the *unmarked* stem valves should be checked with a valve mirror.

1. Remove the piston adjacent to the valve being checked.

2. Insert the valve mirror (Figure 77) and check the ports in both the "down" and "up" positions.

3. Add cork washers or felt washers under the valve cap and finger button (or top valve caps) as needed.

NOTE: Valves with special corks and anticlick devices should be sent to a repairman who has factory parts.

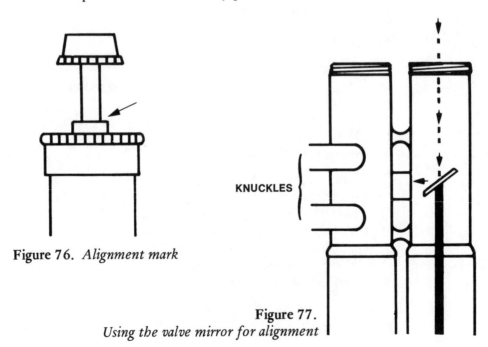

Figure 76. *Alignment mark*

KNUCKLES

Figure 77.
Using the valve mirror for alignment

Adjusting the Valve Spring Tension

A set of valve springs is inexpensive. For repair, the best solution is to buy and install new springs.

For instructions on temporary spring adjustment, see Emergency Repairs, page 152.

Removing Bell Tubing Dents

(List E Tools)

For removing dents that are located between the bell flare and the bell tubing curve, follow these procedures:

1. Clamp the large end of the tapered steel mandrel *tightly* in the vise.
2. Slip the bell over the mandrel.
3. With a rolling action, push out the dents.
4. Push out small, stubborn dents with the tip of the mandrel.

Removing Obstructions from Tubing

(List A Tools)

On the larger instruments these objects can usually be removed by rotating the instrument while jarring it with the hand. On smaller instruments a flexible rod must be used.

1. Pull all the affected slides.
2. Insert the rod in the small end of the bore.
3. Push toward the larger bore.

   CAUTION: Inserting the flexible rod through a valve casing can cause damage to the casing wall. If this procedure is necessary, the instrument should be sent to a repair shop.

4. A wedged coin can often pivot like a gate and allow the rod to pass through as though there were no obstruction. In this case, repeated movements of the rod will be necessary to remove it.
5. Strong water pressure from a flexible hose may also be used, especially on the larger brasses.

FIBERGLASS PROBLEMS

(Acetone, epoxy glue, disposable rags, small brushes, soap and water)

NOTE: Since the various brands of fiberglass sousaphones have differing designs, braces, and finishes, the director or instrumentalist should use discretion in attempting fiberglass repairs other than those listed in Emergency Repairs, page 152. Also, the braces that attach the brass valve section to the fiberglass tubings on some sousaphone models have specially designed nuts, threaded rods, braces, and set screws for disconnecting the valve section. If broken, these should be replaced with factory parts or sent to a repairman who is equipped and capable of making these parts in keeping with the design of the instrument. Makeshift repairs (such as soldering braces that are designed to attach by set screws or nuts) often damage the finish and make disconnecting the valve section difficult, or cause more expensive repairs later.

Fiberglass timpani problems should be sent to the factory.

Cleaning

CAUTION: Tests by some authorities indicate that chemicals involving prolonged contact with the skin or inhalation of the fumes of acetone or other liquids used with polyester resins can be absorbed into the bloodstream. In addition, these liquids are highly flammable. Use them only in a well ventilated area and with gloves or thickly padded cloths.

1. Detach the brass section from the fiberglass section. (Some lacquer finishes can be damaged by acetone.)

2. Dampen a cloth with acetone and clean a small area at a time. Even the most stubborn scuff marks will disappear with little effort.

3. Clean the acetone residue with soap and water and dry with a clean cloth.

Reattaching Loose Sockets, Spuds, or Flanges

1. Disconnect the rod or bracket from the socket, **spud**, or flange.

2. Clean the areas to be glued with acetone.

3. Mix a small amount of epoxy glue according to directions and apply to both surfaces.

4. Place the socket, spud, or flange in the correct position and remove the excess glue.

5. Allow twenty-four hours for drying.

6. Reassemble the rod or bracket.

NOTE: If the socket, spud, or flange has been broken from the fiber-glass tubing so that its position and angle for reattachment are obvious, the brass valve section should be disconnected for easier access for gluing. If not, the brass valve section should be in position and the rod or bracket should be attached to the glued part during the drying process.

ROTARY VALVE INSTRUMENTS

Restringing the Valves

(List A Tools and Supplies)

1. Cut the string an inch or two longer than needed.

2. Tie a large knot at one end.

3. Insert the string through the hole nearest the lever.

4. Wind the string around the post, and loop it under the **stop arm string screw** (Figure 78).

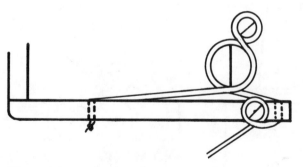

Figure 78. *Stringing the rotary valve*

5. Check the lever and make sure that it is level with the other levers.

6. Tighten the stop arm string screw.

7. Insert the string in the hole at the end of the key arm.

8. Loop the string around the string screw (see Figure 78).

9. Tighten the string screw.

10. Adjust for loose action as needed.

11. Remove the excess string.

Installing New Bumper Corks

(List A Tools and Supplies)

1. Remove the old cork.

2. Push the cork into the cork groove in the **stop plate** (Figure 79).

3. Cut the cork off even with the top of the stop plate.

4. Remove the bottom valve cap.

5. Depress and release the valve key and check the alignment marks (see Figure 27, page 39).

6. Slice off the edge of the cork that contacts the stop arm (Figure 80) until the alignment marks coincide.

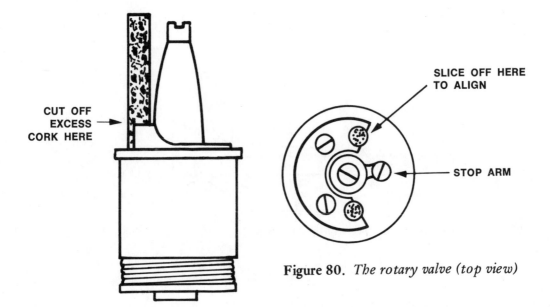

CUT OFF
EXCESS
CORK HERE

SLICE OFF HERE
TO ALIGN

STOP ARM

Figure 80. *The rotary valve (top view)*

Figure 79.
Installing new bumper cork (side view)

Repairing Stuck Valves (Rotors)

(List A Tools and Supplies)

If a valve is stuck, *do not* try to unstick it by forcing the key down. Bent levers, broken strings, or "scored" bearings are often the result.

1. Remove the string.

2. Remove the valve cap.

3. "Back off" the **stop arm** screw about 1/16 inch (Figure 81).

4. Place the open palm under the valve to catch the bearing washer and valve (rotor).

5. Tap lightly on the stop arm screw (Figure 81) until the valve is released.

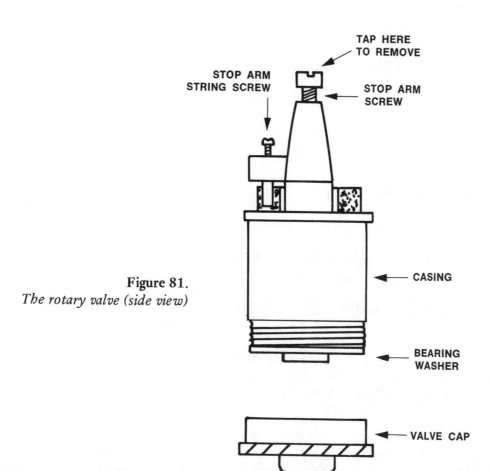

Figure 81.
The rotary valve (side view)

6. Remove the stop arm screw.

7. Clean the stems and the bearing holes with a nonabrasive brass polish.

8. Wash the valve and the bearing holes with soap and water to remove the polish residue.

9. Oil the valve bearing points and replace in the casing with the long stem first.

10. Oil the bearing washer hole and place it over the stem and casing so that the casing and bearing washer marks are aligned (see Figure 27, page 39).

11. Use the rawhide mallet or a soft wooden block to tap the bearing washer evenly into the casing.

12. With the fingers, check the valve action by twisting the long stem.

13. If the valve is not free, tap lightly on different areas of the bearing washer until it becomes free.

14. Replace the valve cap, the stop arm, and screw.

15. Restring.

NOTE: Do not attempt further repairs if the valve is still not free. Send the instrument to a repair shop.

Leveling the Keys

(List A Tools)

1. Release the pressure on the stop arm string screw.

2. Move the key to the desired position.

3. Tighten the stop arm string screw.

TROMBONES

Removing Stuck Tapers

(List B Tools)

On most trombones, the bell and slide sections join with a tapered tube that is held together by a locknut. Occasionally these will become wedged. Do *not* exert excessive pressure in trying to release them. Broken soldered joints and twisted tubings can result.

1. Insert the wedges between the shoulders of the two joints (Figure 82).

2. Tap lightly until the joints separate.

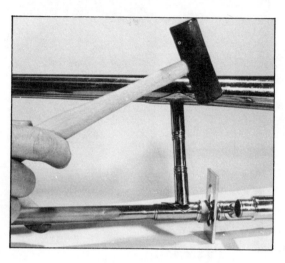

Figure 82.
Removing stuck tapers

Repairing Hand Slide Problems

1. Dented outer slides (List C Tools)
   a) Place the trombone slide mandrel in the vise and wipe it clean.
   b) Remove the outer (hand) slides and slip the dented slide over the mandrel.
   c) Using the small dent hammer, tap lightly on the edge of the dents.
   d) Test the slide for sticking.
   e) Repeat as needed.

2. Nonparallel inner slide (No equipment is necessary)
   a) Insert one of the inner slides into its companion outer slide, leaving the other inner slide free (Figure 83).
   b) If the "free" inner slide is not parallel with its companion outer slide, grasp the "free" slide *near the cork barrel* and bend it until it is aligned properly with the outer slide (Figure 84).

3. Nonparallel outer slides (List C Tools)
   a) Using the vernier caliper, measure the distance between the

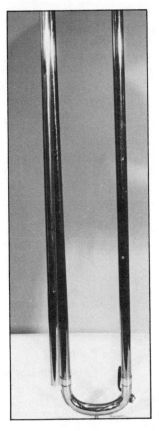

Figure 83.
*Nonparallel
inner slide*

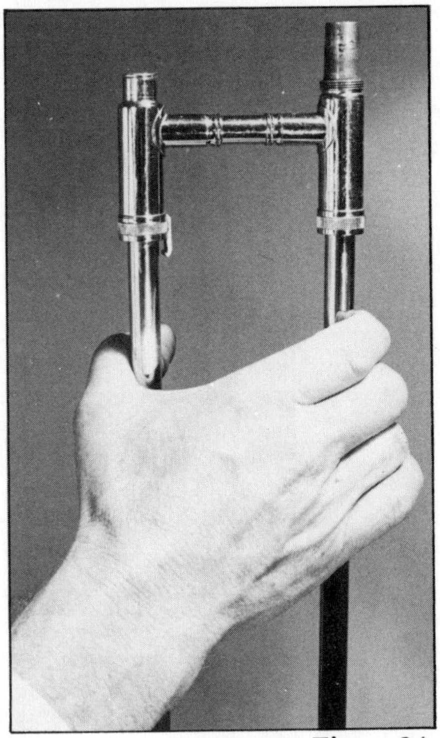

Figure 84.
Bending the inner slide

outer slides near the hand slide bow and at the other end near
the hand slide crossbar.

b) If the slides are not parallel, use *only* hand or finger pressure to
bend the bow in the direction necessary to make the slides
parallel (Figures 85 and 86).

c) Repeat Number 2 above and realign the inner and outer slides.

d) If the slides still "bind," the problem is obviously in the soldered portions of the crossbar (send it to the repair shop) or
else the cause is one of the problems to follow.

4. Warped slides (A clean, flat table)

a) Wipe the dust from the testing surface.

b) Pull the inner slides free from the outer slides and lay them on
the flat surface. Note which side is off the surface.

c) Using the hand and wrist, grasp the inner slides near the crossbar and twist in a direction opposite to the warp (Figure 87).

d) Lay the slide on the surface and check.

e) Test the outer (hand) slides in the same manner on the flat surface.

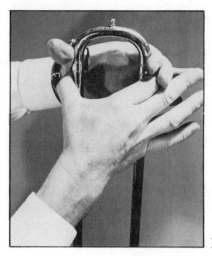

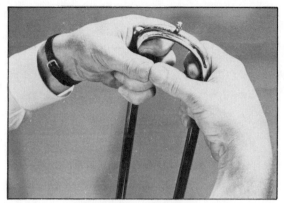

Figure 86. *Widening the slide bow*

Figure 85. *Narrowing the slide bow*

f)   To straighten the outer slides, grasp the slide bow in one hand and the slide crossbar in the other.
g)   Twist *lightly* in a direction opposite to the warp (Figure 88).
h)   Test, and repeat as needed.

CAUTION: If the outer slide (hand slide) is badly warped, it should be unsoldered and realigned by a repairman.

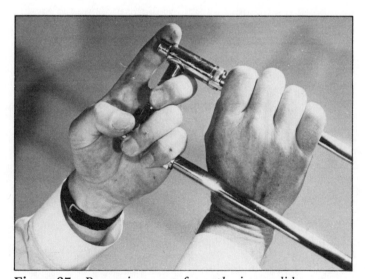

Figure 87. *Removing warp from the inner slide*

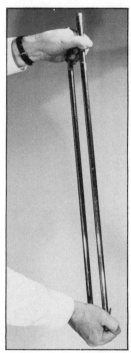

Figure 88.
Removing warp from the outer slide

5. Bowed slides (No equipment is necessary)

    NOTE: Bowed slides often occur when a player inserts the tuning slide into the bell section while the trombone is "standing" on the slide bow knob. With a little patience and practice, the director can straighten the bowed slide without expense.

    a) Remove the hand slide from the inner slides.
    b) "Sight" down the slide toward the light to determine in which direction the slide is bowed.
    c) Holding the slide rigid by the crossbar (hand slide bar), rest the slide bow knob on the end of a solid table or desk (Figure 89).
    d) *Lightly* rub the palm of the other hand over the bowed area.
    e) "Sight" down the slide.
    f) Repeat as needed until the slides appear to be straight.
    g) Test the hand slide with the inner slides.

NOTE: Though procedures 1 through 5 above represent rather delicate repair techniques, the director who is conscientious and careful in his efforts can successfully eliminate many repair problems without costly mistakes.

6. Pitted stockings (List A Supplies)
    Storing the trombone for summer vacations without proper *cleaning and drying* will often result in the formation of stubborn depos-

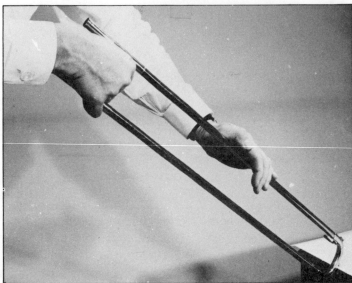

Figure 89.
*Straightening
a bowed slide*

its and/or pitted areas on the stockings. Once this has happened, the player must contend with poor slides as long as he plays the instrument. The problem can be eliminated only by having new slides installed. A temporary but helpful remedy follows:

a) With a nonabrasive metal polish, clean the deposits from the stockings.

b) Using a rigid trombone cleaning rod (as described in Chapter 1, "Trombone Cleaning," page 12), apply the polish to the end of the cloth and polish the inside of the hand slides; especially the bottom, where the stockings are located when the slide is in first position.

c) Clean both the inner slides and the hand slides with soap and water and rinse thoroughly.

d) Since pitted stockings will often give trouble when slide oil is used, cold cream and water should be used for more satisfactory slide action.

Freeing the Stuck Tuning Slide

(List A Tools and Supplies)

1. Saturate the inner and outer tubing with penetrating oil and let stand overnight.

2. Try to remove the slide as shown in Figure 90.

Figure 90. *Unsticking the tuning slide*

3. If the slide is not free, alternately tap on the ends of the crossbar (or brace) with the rawhide mallet until both slides are loose.

4. Polish the slides with a nonabrasive brass polish.

5. Clean the slides with soap and water.

6. Grease the slides independently and in a spiralling motion coat each slide wall thoroughly.

7. Replace the tuning slide as shown in Figure 91.

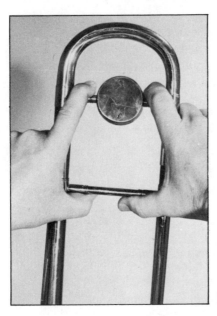

Figure 91. *Installing the tuning slide*

Freeing the Stuck Valve

Follow the procedures for Rotary Valve Instruments, pages 113-114.

Replacing Slide Bumper Corks

(List E Tools and Supplies)

1. Unscrew the slide locking arm from the cork barrel.

2. Slip the cork removing tool over the inner slide and push its hooked tip into the cork barrel (Figure 92).

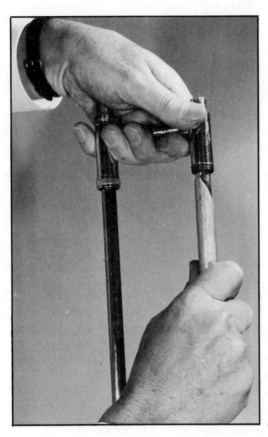

Figure 92.
Removing bumper cork

3. Twist the tool to the right (twist to the left when using the large bore cork removing tool) while simultaneously pulling away from the cork barrel.

4. Repeat Number 3 above until *all* cork (sometimes felt) is removed.

5. Cut a strip of 3/32-inch cork the same width as the old cork.

6. Using the dent hammer and jeweler's anvil, hammer the cork to make it supple.

7. Wrap the strip of cork around the slide, cut it to length, and insert it in the cork barrel.

8. Use the butt end of the cork removing tool to push the bumper to the bottom of the cork barrel.

9. Test with the slide lock for correct thickness.

10. Repeat the above procedures for the other slide.

PERCUSSIONS
Drums

Installing New Heads

When new heads are to be installed on a bass drum, timpano, snare drum, timbale, conga, tom-tom, cocktail drum, or bongo, a few basic steps should be followed:

1. Release the tension on the screws (one turn per screw) in a clockwise motion around the drum.

2. Check the rim for cuts, dents, and raised wood grain.

3. Sand the rim with a fine garnet or waterproof paper.

4. Coat the rim *lightly* with paraffin, graphite, or powdered talc.

5. Grease the tension screws *lightly* with mutton tallow or a light petroleum grease.

6. Check the hoop for dirt and rough areas.

7. Place the hoop on the drum and tighten each screw in a clockwise motion, one turn at a time.

NOTE: Some percussionists prefer tightening on opposite sides. Use the method recommended by a percussion instructor.

8. Check the head to see that it is level.

9. Test the head near each screw for tuning.

Installing New Hardware

New **lugs**, mufflers, **snare butts**, drum key holders, and accessory brackets can be purchased for all brands of percussions, and they are easily installed.

1. Remove one of the heads.

2. Remove the old device (if replacing) by unscrewing it from inside the shell.

3. Install the new device, making certain that the mounting screws are equipped with lock washers and are tightened snugly.

4. For installing a new device, locate the desirable position for it on the shell, then mark and drill the holes.

5. Install as in Number 3 above.

Mallet Instruments

Replacing Worn Glockenspiel Grommets

(List A Tools)

New grommets can be purchased through a local music dealer or direct from the factory. Bent or worn bar-retaining screws and new backing felt, if needed, should also be ordered at the same time.

1. Remove the screws from each bar. Some bar-retaining screws have a three-way locking security—two locknuts plus a threaded hole in the mounting rail.

2. Clean the mounting rail or backing felt.

3. Check the mounting rail for looseness against the frame.

4. Clean each bar.

5. Replace and check each bar for a clear response.

Other Mallet Repairs

Major repairs on other mallet instruments should be left to the factory. The only exception is the replacement of drive belts (vibes) when a list of factory instructions is available.

Cymbals

Cracked cymbals can be repaired to give temporary service.

1. Drill a hole at the end of the crack.

2. Saw away a portion, as shown in Figure 93.

3. Smooth the edges.

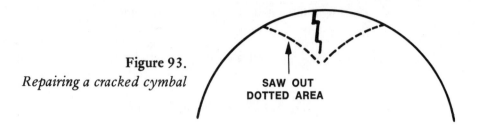

Figure 93.
Repairing a cracked cymbal

SUMMARY

Many problems that occur in an average band have been omitted from this chapter because the necessary equipment and repair skills are not available to most band directors. The following repairs should be handled only by a competent repairman who has the proper equipment:

1. Unsoldered braces
2. Broken keys
3. Broken tenons
4. Broken woodwind bodies
5. Cracked woodwind bodies
6. Major dents
7. Key **swedging**
8. Burnishing
9. Shortening clarinet barrel joints
10. Installing tenon caps
11. Installing floor pegs on bass clarinets
12. Tenon reaming
13. Mouthpiece refacing
14. Buffing
15. Lacquering
16. Major work on piston or rotary valves
17. Timpani pedal repairs
18. Making hinge rods

19. Straightening hinge rods

20. Unpinning flute hinge rods

21. Acid cleaning mouthpieces

22. **Pickling** brass instruments

23. Removing lacquer

24. Removing threaded octave tubes

Most Frequent Problems 5

The purpose of this chapter is to give the director, instrumentalist, or student repairman a list of problems that are encountered most frequently in order of probability. This does not, however, negate the importance of the preceding chapters. Straightening a bent key, for instance, will not solve a problem completely if a pad is leaking elsewhere.

Also bear in mind that this chapter, and others, will not solve all the problems that can occur on band instruments. The length of time one should devote to solving a knotty problem must, therefore, be left to the judgment of the user of this book.

SPECIAL CAUTION: If a pad is seated improperly due to a bent key or pad cut, *do not* place a pad slick or **leveling wedge** against a tone hole on wooden and plastic instruments to bend the key or cup properly. Severe damage to the tone hole can occur from this procedure. To straighten, use flatnosed pliers with smooth jaws and bend as shown in Figure 94.

Figure 94. *Straightening a key*

PICCOLO

1. Loose pads

    Cause: Most piccolo pads must be **floated in** for proper seating.
    After a year or more of use, the pad cement becomes
    dry and brittle and will fall out from rough handling or
    after getting wet.

    Solution: See Chapter 4, Piccolo Padding, page 61.

2. Improperly operating bridge keys

    Cause: Shims (used in adjusting bridge keys) have fallen out, or
    a pad cup is bent.

    Solution: a) Check visually, and with a feeler, to determine if
    one pad is touching the tone hole more heavily than
    the other.

    b) Estimate the thickness of paper or cork that will be
    necessary for use as a shim.

    c) Slip the paper or cork under the overlapping plateau
    (Figure 95), press the key down, and check for
    equal pressure. Try different thicknesses of paper or

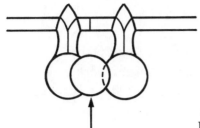

Figure 95. *The piccolo plateau*

cork, or use two or more pieces of paper (or paper *and* cork) until equal pressure is indicated.
d) Cut the shim(s) needed into a small segment(s) that will not protrude from the overlapping plateau.
e) With a needle spring or toothpick, place a *small* amount of glue to the shim and press it to the underside of the plateau.
f) Check the pads with a feeler. Recheck by playing that particular note using light finger pressure.

NOTE: Do *not* attempt to straighten a bent cup or key on a piccolo. Send it to a repair shop.

3. Clicking keys
   Cause: Missing cork(s), bent key(s), bent post(s), or improperly bent spring(s).
   Solution: For missing corks follow the procedures in Chapter 4, Corking Keys, page 54. Other problems of clicking keys should not be attempted by a novice.

4. Damaged tenon on head joint
   Cause: Accidents, improper handling, etc.
   Solution: Use a piccolo tenon expander (see Figure 59, page 81) and a small dent hammer, with light taps. If a piccolo tenon expander is not available, send the instrument to a repair shop.

5. Leaking tuning cork
   Cause: Age, excessive heat, poor job of installation, etc.
   Solution: See Chapter 4, Replacing Head Corks, page 77.

6. Leaking or unsoldered lip plate
   Cause: Accident or improper handling.
   Solution: Resoldering should be done by an experienced repairman.

FLUTE

1. Bridge from low C to C♯ not adjusted properly

    Cause: Bent spatula on C♯ or missing cork on key.

    Solution: See Chapter 4, Adjusting Bridge Keys, No. 4, page 80, and Figure 96.

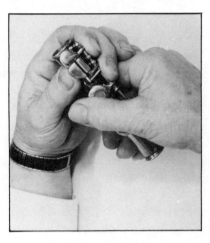

Figure 96. *Adjusting the low C♯*

2. Notes will not respond below third line B

    Cause: Hinge rod for first finger C has unscrewed slightly from constantly fingering C, and its pivot point that inserts into the B♭ key is too loose to allow the B♭ key to seat properly.

    Solution: Place clear fingernail polish on the slotted end (that fits into the post) and screw up tightly; or *slightly* flatten the slotted end (Figure 97) so that it will fit snugly and not unscrew.

3. F will not respond properly

    Cause: a) Forked B♭ arm is making the B♭ key seat before the F♯ key.

    b) The adjusting screw to F♯ has unscrewed.

    c) F and/or F♯ pads are not seated properly.

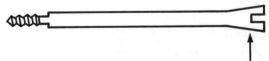

Figure 97. *The flattened hinge rod for upper C (exaggerated)*

d) G$\sharp$ key has been bent, allowing a leak.

Solution: a, b) See Standard Repairs chapter, Adjusting Bridge Keys, Number 2, page 79.

c) See Standard Repairs chapter, Installing and Seating Flute Pads, page 58.

d) See Figure 94, page 128.

4. Flute will play only one harmonic note

Cause: A trill key pad is open, a trill key pad is missing, or is leaking badly.

Solution: An open key usually implies a disconnected needle spring, a bent post, or a bent or rusted hinge rod. If the problem is a loose spring, reconnect it to the spring block with a spring hook. If a pad is worn or missing, see Chapter 4, Installing Glued Pads, pages 55-56. If a post or the long trill rod is bent or frozen by rust, send the instrument to a repair shop.

5. All notes respond poorly

Cause: a) Leaking tuning cork.

b) Leaking lip plate.

c) Pad skins have deteriorated.

Solution: a) See Standard Repairs chapter, Replacing Head Corks, pages 77-78.

b) An unsoldered or leaking lip plate should be re-soldered by an experienced repairman.

c) See Chapter 4, Installing and Seating Flute Pads, pages 58-59.

6. Key(s) does not open properly

Cause: a) Unhooked or broken spring.

b) Bent post.

c) Rusted, bent, or frozen hinge rod.

d) Binding pivot screw.

Solution: a) Rehook or replace (See Chapter 4, Replacing Needle Springs, page 65).

b) See Chapter 4, Eliminating Sluggish Key Action, Number 4, page 73.

c) Do not attempt this repair.

d) Check for a bent post and follow solution (b) above. If none of the above are causes, use a pivot screw reamer as directed in Chapter 4, Relieving Pivot Screw Pressure, page 71.

7. "Sticking" sound when pads open

Cause: Sugar contents in breath moisture have accumulated on the pad.

Solution: Slip a leaf of eyeglass cleaning paper under the pad, depress the key lightly, and pull the leaf out. Repeat as needed.

8. "Clicking" sound when playing A

Cause: a) Improper corking of the F$\sharp$ foot, causing F$\sharp$ to open too far, hitting the B$\flat$ trill lever.

   b) The B$\flat$ (on some models the thumb B) trill lever has been bent and is hitting against the F$\sharp$ cup.

Solution: a) Recork or add a shim to the foot to close the F key slightly.

   b) Bend the trill arm up slightly.

9. Bridge notes (F$\sharp$, A, and forked B$\flat$) do not respond

Cause: Loose adjusting screws (F$\sharp$), or an unscrewed C hinge rod (A, B$\flat$).

Solution: Adjust until equal pressure exists between the companion pads and seal the screws with clear fingernail polish. Flatten the C rod as in Number 2 above and as shown in Figure 97, page 130.

OBOE—ENGLISH HORN

1. Notes do not respond properly below third space C$\sharp$

Cause: a) The bridge key (upper joint) to the forked B$\flat$ and C has been bent and is holding the small pads for B$\flat$ and C open.

   b) One or both trill keys are open, pads are not seated properly, or pads are leaking badly.

Solution: a) Rebend the bridge key so that there is a slight clearance between the lower and the upper joint bridges to B$\flat$ and C.

   b) Check the pads for leaks or for incorrect seating; check for broken needle springs, binding pivot screws, bent hinge rods, or twisted posts, and follow the repair techniques listed in Chapter 4 for appropriate correction.

2. Notes do not respond below second line G

   Cause: a) The adjusting screws on the right-hand stack are not adjusted properly.

   b) The bridge from the F♯ to the G♯ pad (Figure 98) is contacting the G♯ before allowing the F♯ pad to seat.

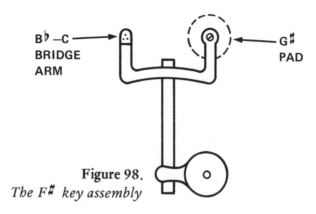

Figure 98.
The F♯ key assembly

   Solution: a) Set the adjusting screws for proper tension between the companion pads and seal the screws with clear fingernail polish.

   b) Recork the F♯-G♯ bridge with thinner cork, adjust the screw, or rebend the arm so that the F♯ pad has proper seating pressure while maintaining enough pressure on the bridge arm to prevent the G♯ pad from opening when depressing the G♯ lever.

3. Low B and B♭ do not close together when depressing the low B♭ spatula

   Cause: One (sometimes more) of the three bridge adjustment points (Figure 99) is not functioning correctly.

   Solution: a) Check the low B♭ bridge (Number 3 point) for incorrect corking or damage to one or both bridge arms.

   b) Check the adjusting screw (Number 2 point) by tightening (or loosening) to secure equal pressure between the low B and B♭ pads.

   NOTE: The large, flat spring under the adjusting screw on the opposite arm of point 2 keeps the D♯ (E♭) key closed except when fingering D♯. If the adjusting screw

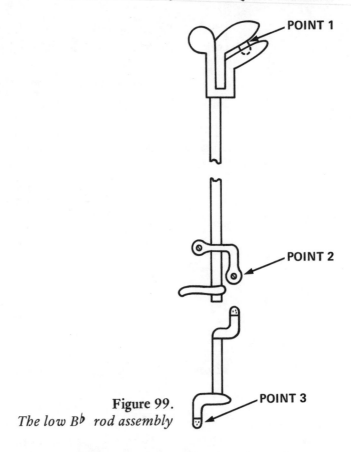

Figure 99.
The low B♭ rod assembly

on point 2 is tightened too much, the other screw will press the large spring and allow the weaker, flat spring on the D♯ key to open the key slightly and prevent correct response on all notes below D♯ . If correct adjustment cannot be made from this point, make adjustments from points 1 and 3.

c)   Recork or bend the extension arm from the B spatula (Number 1 point) to equalize pressure between the B and B♭ pads.

4.   Low C (and sometimes B and B♭) responds an octave higher

Cause: a)   The arm and/or adjusting screw from low B and B♭ to D♯ is holding the D♯ key open slightly. (See the note on Number 3 solution above.)

b)   The needle spring on the low C♯ lever rod (Figure 100) is too weak to override the flat spring on the C♯ key, thus allowing a leak in the C♯ pad.

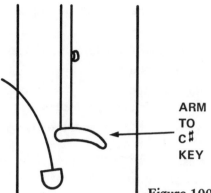

Figure 100. *The override spring to low C♯ key*

Solution: a) Loosen the adjusting screw to the D♯ (E♭) spring and make low B and B♭ adjustments from points 1 and 3 (see 3-b above), or bend the tip of the large flat spring under the D♯ key so that there is a slight clearance between the spring and the low B-B♭ rod arm.

b) Bend the needle spring for the C♯ lever rod to give more tension in holding the C♯ key closed (Figure 100).

BASSOON

NOTE: Many problems of leaking pads, improper bridge key operations, or bent keys and rods can be avoided by learning to assemble and disassemble the joints properly. A contributing factor to bent keys is tenons that are too tight or are not lubricated properly.

1. A leaking pad on the whisper or **piano key**
    Cause: Incorrect procedure when inserting or removing the bocal, causing the pad to fray, or the pad is seated incorrectly.

    Solution: Follow the instructions in Chapter 4, Installing Glued Pads, pages 55-56. If a kid skin pad is used, puncturing will be unnecessary.

2. The whisper key does not close properly
    Cause: One or more of the intricate bridge mechanisms is bent, or is adjusted improperly.

Solution: Straighten the rod, key, lever, or flat spring, or else re-cork or retube where needed.

3. The keys (usually low B♭, B, C, and D) operated by the left thumb on the bass joint do not close simultaneously

Cause: Improper assembly, dry tenons, missing corks or felts, or improperly tempered metal in the keys or levers.

Solution: Using a leak light, adjust the bridge mechanisms as follows:
a) Check the closed pads (C♯, D♯) for proper seating.
b) Check the low D pad for proper seating.
c) Check the low C pad for proper seating.
d) Check the low C and D pads for simultaneous clos-ing. Bend the spring arm (usually on the low D spatula) to effect equal closing.
e) Check the low B pad for proper seating.
f) Press the low B spatula and adjust so that the B, C, and D pads close simultaneously.
g) Check the bell B♭ pad for proper seating.
h) On some bassoons the bell B♭ key is operated separately from B, C, and D. If the bassoon is de-signed so that the B♭ spatula closes the B♭, C, and D keys simultaneously, adjust (by corking or bend-ing) so that the B♭ spatula closes all four.

4. Leak(s) in the boot or butt joint

Cause: a) Leaking end bow.
b) Dried and leaking pads.
c) Improperly operating bridge mechanisms.
d) Bent keys, rods, or pad cups.

Solution: a) See Chapter 4, Recorking the End Bow, page 90.
b) Replacing some pads in the boot joint can be very frustrating and sometimes damaging to the tone holes, **action rods**, and keys. If the novice repairman wants to attempt this repair, he should use bassoon pads and follow the procedures given in Chapter 4, Installing Glued Pads, pages 55-56, in combina-tion with a small leak light.
c) Adjusting bridge keys on the boot joint is also a delicate procedure due to the four action rods that operate through the body. It is not recommended for the inexperienced repairman.
d) Rebend the keys, rods, and pad cups by using

smooth-jawed, flatnosed pliers only. Do *not* place a pad slick or leveling wedge under the pad cup and against the tone hole.

5. Leaks in the tenor joint

Cause: a) Poor or unseated pads.
  b) Bent keys or rods.
  c) Damaged tone holes.

Solution: a) Replacing or reseating pads in this joint is left to the judgment of the director, instrumentalist, or student repairman. If attempted, use kid skin pads, install and seat as in clarinet pad seating. A leak light with a small bulb is helpful.
  b) See 4-d above.
  c) Let an experienced repairman handle damaged tone holes in bassoons.

SOPRANO CLARINETS

1. Forked E♭ -B♭ does not respond correctly

Cause: a) Improper assembly has bent the bridge or removed the cork on the second ring key (see Figure 119, page 193).
  b) The tenon needs recorking.

Solution: a) Recork or rebend (Figure 101) the upper joint bridge for simultaneous closing of the E♭ -B♭ key (upper joint) and the B♭ -F key (lower joint).
  b) See Chapter 4, Corking Tenons, page 61.

2. Pressing the left-hand low E lever or the right-hand low E spatula produces a squeak or squeal when playing the third line B or the low E (Chalumeau)

Cause: a) The low E and/or the low F pad is not seated correctly.
  b) The crow foot (or presser foot) is not corked properly.
  c) The low E spatula is not closing the low E and F pads simultaneously.

Solution: a) See Chapter 4, Seating Glued Pads . . . , pages 56-57.
  b) See Chapter 4, Corking Keys, page 54.

Figure 101.
Adjusting the upper bridge (Clarinet)

    c)   If the low E touches the tone hole first, bend the low E spatula down while holding the pad arm up (Figure 102). Reverse this procedure if the low F touches the tone hole first. Check for equal pressure with a feeler.

3. Clicking sound in the left-hand levers
    Cause: a)   The levers are bent.
                 b)   The levers or the arms to the levers are not corked properly.
                 c)   The silencer skins are worn or missing.

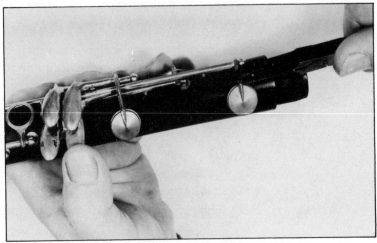

Figure 102. *Adjusting the low E-F (Clarinet)*

Solution: a) Straighten with flatnosed pliers.
               b) Recork as needed.
               c) See Chapter 4, Installing Silencer Skins, page 85.

4. Clicking on all other keys
    Cause: Missing corks or bent keys.
    Solution: Recork or rebend.

5. Notes below the third finger, left hand, will not respond
    Cause: a) The $C\sharp$-$G\sharp$ key or the bridge key for the forked
                     $E\flat$-$B\flat$ is bent, preventing the $C\sharp$-$G\sharp$ key from
                     closing properly.
             b) The spring for $C\sharp$-$G\sharp$ is unhooked or broken.
             c) The bridge key for the forked $E\flat$-$B\flat$ is corked or
                     adjusted improperly and will not allow the $B\flat$-F
                     (third ring key) pad to close.
    Solution: a) Rebend the problem key, then check the $C\sharp$-$G\sharp$
                     pad for seating and the bridge keys for simultaneous
                     closings.
             b) See Chapter 4, Replacing Needle Springs, page
                     65.
             c) See Chapter 4, Adjusting the Bridge Key, page 86,
                     and Figure 101.

6. Fuzzy sound on the notes as listed below

NOTE: A mature player who "fills" the clarinet with much breath
support is apt to experience this problem. Although most fuzzy notes
can be eliminated by opening the key further, the player will need to
adjust slightly for proper intonation.

    A. Low G (Chalumeau)
       Cause: The F pad is too thick or the F key is not opening
                     far enough.
       Solution: Send the clarinet to a good repairman with a note
                     stating the problem. The solution requires a deli-
                     cate adjustment that involves other keys.

    B. Chromatic B-$F\sharp$, Chromatic $E\flat$-$B\flat$, $C\sharp$-$G\sharp$
       Cause: The keys are not opening far enough.
       Solution: Sand the cork, recork with thinner cork, or bend
                     the key arm or spatula to allow the key to open
                     further.

   C. C-G and E-B
      Cause: The keys are not opening far enough.
      Solution: Sand the cork under the third ring key (Figure 119, page 193) foot or recork with thinner cork. This will eliminate the buzz in both pads.

   D. Throat A♭, A, and B♭
      Cause: Cork under one or more of the keys (usually the A♭) is too thick, the thumb key or the A♭ spatula is bent, or the tone hole(s) is dirty.
      Solution: If recorking, rebending, or cleaning the tone holes (and register tube) do not eliminate the buzz, send the clarinet to the repair shop with a note stating the problem. Poor throat tones are inherent in most clarinets and the player must contend with this problem. If the notes are unbearably poor and the brand or model justifies correction, send the clarinet to the factory or to a repairman who specializes in the clarinet. Reboring or undercutting the tone hole(s) is sometimes necessary.

   E. Side key(s) in the upper joint
      Cause: A frayed or poor pad, a bent key, or incorrect cork.
      Solution: Repad, rebend, or recork the key(s) as needed.

   F. Poor sound on all notes below throat A♭
      Cause: The adjusting screw on A♭ to A is too tight.
      Solution: Loosen to the correct setting and seal with clear fingernail polish.

ALTO AND BASS CLARINETS

As there are many brands, models, and designs of the large clarinets, simple solutions cannot be given for every problem that will arise on these unpredictable instruments. The only problems listed will be those that can be solved by a novice repairman. Unless other problems are identical with those of a soprano clarinet, send the large clarinet to a repair shop.

   1. Improper response when playing throat B♭, or when using the register key

Cause: a) New Models: Improper adjustment of the screws to the **sickle,** to the thumb lever, or to the upper register pad.

b) Old Models: Improper adjustment of the bridge rods from the third finger, right hand, to the register key.

c) Improper corking.

Solution: a) Adjust the screws so that the large pad (usually under the thumb lever) opens when playing throat B♭ and the small pad (the uppermost pad) closes. In playing all other notes using the register key, the large pad should close and the small pad should be open.

b) See Chapter 4, Alto and Bass Clarinets, Octave or Register Key Problems, page 88.

c) Follow the standard corking procedures.

2. Clicking levers (left hand)

Cause: a) Silencer skins are worn or missing.

b) Levers are bent.

Solution: a) See Chapter 4, Installing Silencer Skins in Lever Keys, page 85.

b) See Chapter 4, Rebending Keys, page 64.

3. Notes will not respond below the first line E

Cause: a) Improper bridge adjustment on C, D, or E.

b) Brittle and leaking pads.

c) Missing felt under the plateau key.

Solution: a) See Chapter 4, Adjusting the Bridge Key, page 90.

b) See Chapter 4, Installing Glued Pads, page 55, and Seating Glued Pads, page 56. On most large clarinets it is possible to seat each bridge pad separately by removing a companion bridge key. After seating each pad separately, the bridge may be adjusted for unison closings.

c) Install a key felt with pad and cork cement.

SAXOPHONES

1. Bent octave teeter (inoperative octave mechanism)

Cause: Failure to insert an end plug into the tenon socket when placing the saxophone in the case (Figure 103).

Solution: Bend to the correct operating position (See Chapter 4, Adjusting the Octave Mechanism, page 92, and Figure 104).

Figure 104. *Straightening the octave bridge*

Figure 103. *Inserting the end plug*

2. G♯ does not open

   Cause: a) An unhooked or broken spring.
            b) Saliva residue from improper swabbing.

   Solution: a) Rehook or replace the spring (see Chapter 4, Replacing Needle Springs, page 65).
             b) See Chapter 4, Repairing the Sticking G♯ Pad, page 100.

3. Difficulty in playing low B and B♭

   Cause: a) The G♯ key is opening slightly.
            b) The low D♯, C, B, B♭, or C♯ pads are faulty or not seated properly.
            c) The bridge B♭ to B is not adjusted properly.
            d) The cork on the G♯ lever foot is too thick, preventing the B and B♭ from closing.

   Solution: a) See Chapter 4, Adjusting the Bridge Mechanisms, Number 4, page 99.

b) See Chapter 4, Seating Glued Pads (Saxophones), page 57.
c) See Chapter 4, Adjusting the Bridge Mechanisms, Number 8, page 100.
d) Cut or sand the cork foot.

4. Low notes tend to play an octave higher
   Cause: a) Improper operation of the octave mechanism.
   b) A leaking neck tenon.
   c) Leaking pads in the palm keys.
   d) Unsoldered tone holes.
   Solution: a) See Chapter 4, Adjusting the Octave Mechanism, page 92, Figure 60, page 92, and Figure 104.
   b) Tighten the neck tension screw or expand the neck tenon (see Chapter 4, Expanding the Tenon, page 93).
   c) Locate the problem key(s) with a leak light and re-seat or repad.
   d) Locating and resoldering a tone hole requires experience. If (a), (b), and (c) above do not reveal the problem, send the saxophone to the repair shop.

5. Difficulty in playing the notes listed below

   A. Third line B or second space A
      Cause: The bridge from B to C and A to C is out of adjustment.
      Solution: See Chapter 4, Saxophones, Adjusting the Bridge Mechanisms, Numbers 1 and 2, page 99.

   B. Second line G
      Cause: The spring on the G$\sharp$ lever is broken, unhooked, or weak, the spring under the G$\sharp$ key is too strong, or the cork on the G$\sharp$ lever arm is missing.
      Solution: After locating the exact cause, consult Chapter 4 for the appropriate repair.

   C. First space F
      Cause: An improperly adjusted bridge from F$\sharp$ to G$\sharp$ or B$\flat$
      Solution: Recork, rebend, or adjust the bridge screws.

6. Fluttering sound on any note
   Cause: A loose pad.

Solution: See Installing Glued Pads, page 55, and Seating Glued
Pads (Saxophones), in Chapter 4, page 57.

7. Poor intonation
> *Cause:* a) The mouthpiece is inserted too far onto the neck-
> pipe.
> b) The keys open too far.
> c) This is sometimes inherent in the brand of saxo-
> phone.
>
> *Solution:* a) Recork the neckpipe, if necessary, to allow the
> mouthpiece to fit tightly when placed on the tip of
> the neckpipe.
> b) Add cork or felt to the key feet to close the key
> openings, or send the instrument to a repair shop.
> c) No solution.

8. Fast, heavy vibrato when playing low B♭
> *Cause:* The mouthpiece is not inserted far enough onto the
> neckpipe.
>
> *Solution:* If the saxophone is in tune with the band when the
> vibrato is present, a *possible* solution is to use a weaker
> reed and a loose embouchure with the mouthpiece
> pushed further onto the neckpipe. On some models the
> player must learn to adjust to a compromise position.

9. Sluggish key operation
> *Cause:* a) A rusted pivot screw or hinge rod.
> b) The spring is unhooked, weak, or broken.
> c) A post(s) is bent from accidental dropping or bump-
> ing the instrument, causing binding from a pivot
> screw, hinge rod, key guide, or an adjacent key.
> d) A bent body, causing hinge rod binding.
> e) An incorrect flat spring.
> f) If on the side B♭ , the foot cork key may be too
> thick.
>
> *Solution:* a) Unscrew, clean, and oil.
> b) Rehook or replace (see Chapter 4, Replacing Flat
> Springs and Replacing Needle Springs, page 65).
> c) See Chapter 4, Eliminating Sluggish Key Action,
> Number 4, page 73.
> d, e) Send the instrument to a repair shop.
> f) Sand or cut the cork to allow proper clearance.

10. Fuzzy sound on a given note
> *Cause:* a) The key is not opening far enough.

      b) There is an obstruction in the body.

      c) The octave tube is "stopped up" or damaged.

      d) There is a bent key.

Solution: a) Cut or sand the cork on the key foot.

      b) Open the key that is fuzzy and look into the body for the obstruction.

      c) Remove the octave key and check the tube for dirt or damage. If damaged, send the instrument to a repair shop.

      d) Straighten the key and reseat the pad.

11. Saxophone does not respond clearly on any note

    Cause: An object is lodged in the body.

    Solution: See Chapter 4, Removing Objects from "Stopped Up" Woodwinds, page 75.

12. Chattering sound on one or two notes

    Cause: Sympathetic vibrations caused by a loose **brace**, pivot screw, key guard, or a bent key pressing against an adjacent key or post.

    Solution: Repair the defect according to your qualifications, or send the instrument to a repair shop.

PISTON INSTRUMENTS

1. Stuck mouthpiece

    Cause: Dropping the instrument or making a "popping" sound with the palm of the hand over the mouthpiece.

    Solution: See Chapter 4, Removing Stuck Mouthpieces, page 101.

2. Stuck slides

    Cause: a) Failure to clean and grease them periodically.

      b) A dent in the slide sleeve.

    Solution: a) See Chapter 4, Pulling Stuck Slides, page 104.

      b) Send the instrument to a repair shop.

3. Frozen valve caps

    Cause: Failure to disassemble and clean the instrument periodically.

    Solution: See Chapter 4, Removing Frozen Valve Caps, page 105.

4. Sluggish valves
    Cause: a) Failure to disassemble and clean the instrument
                     periodically.
                 b) A dent in the valve casing.
                 c) Pressure on the casing wall caused by a tuning slide
                     that was bent out-of-line from an accident.
    Solution: a, b, c) See Chapter 4, Freeing Stuck or Sluggish Piston
                 Valves, page 106.

5. Leaking water key
    Cause: Poor cork, a poor spring, a bent water key, or a loose
                 screw.
    Solution: See Chapter 4, Replacing Water Key Corks and Re-
                 placing Water Key Springs, page 103.

6. Bent shank on the mouthpiece
    Cause: Dropping the mouthpiece.
    Solution: See Chapter 4, Straightening Mouthpiece Shanks, page
                 102, and Figure 105.

Figure 105.
Straightening the large mouthpiece shank

7. Leaks in the neckpipe
    Cause: Failure to clean the neckpipe systematically with a
                 flexible brush.
    Solution: Send the instrument to the repair shop for installation
                 of a new neckpipe—a costly but necessary repair.

8. Stuck tuning bits (Sousaphones)
    See Chapter 4, Removing Stuck Tuning Bits, page 105.

ROTARY VALVE INSTRUMENTS

1. Stuck valves
   Cause: Failure to clean and oil the valves properly.
   Solution: See Chapter 4, Repairing Stuck Valves, page 113, and Restringing the Valves, page 111.

2. Collapsed bell flare
   Cause: Placing the bell against the stomach while trying to pull a stubborn slide.
   Solution: Send the instrument to a repair shop.

3. Stuck slides
   Cause: Failure to clean and grease them periodically.
   Solution: See Chapter 4, Pulling Stuck Slides, page 104.

TROMBONES

1. Poor slide action
   Cause: a) Dirty inner and outer slides from failure to clean them often.
                b) Bowed slides.
                c) Dents in the slides.
                d) The slides are not parallel.
                e) Warped slides.
   Solution: a) Clean the slides (both the inner and outer ones) *at least every two weeks* with a flexible brush (see Figure 112, page 189) and with a rigid trombone rod.
                b, c, d, e) See Chapter 4, Repairing Hand Slide Problems, page 115.

2. Leaking water key
   Cause: Poor cork, a poor spring, a bent water key, or a loose screw.
   Solution: See Chapter 4, Replacing Water Key Corks and Replacing Water Key Springs, page 103.

3. Stuck taper
   Cause: Tightening the lock nut too tightly.
   Solution: See Chapter 4, Removing Stuck Tapers, page 114.

Emergency Repairs 6

Occasionally, just prior to a performance, a director will be faced with repair problems that cannot be solved through the use of standard repair practices due to time limitations. In such cases he must take stopgap measures to make the instrument play.

The simplest solution is to have the student borrow an instrument from a band member in a different performance group. A change in instruments is not apt to mar the overall performance except where the student has prepared a solo.

Other corrective measures are listed below but these are only *temporary*. Following the concert or performance, the instrument(s) should be repaired properly, either by a competent repairman or by the director, using the techniques described in the "Standard Repairs" chapter.

It should be noted that in addition to the following list, many of the techniques given in the "Standard Repairs" chapter can be used effectively for emergencies.

WOODWINDS

Loose Pad

Since there will normally be enough glue left in the cup, place the pad in the cup and heat the cup with a match or cigarette lighter until it sticks.

Split or Leaking Pad

Cut a piece of transparent mending tape to the size of the pad. Place the tape over the tone hole with the gummy side up, and press the key.

Loose Tenon (nonmetal)

Wrap dental floss, thread, cotton string, French horn valve cord, paper, or tape around the tenon and grease it.

Loose Tenon (metal)

Wrap one layer of transparent tape around the tenon.

Undersized Saxophone Cork

Wrap the cork with paper or tape until it is large enough for proper tuning.

Broken Spring

Whether the spring is flat or of the needle type, a rubber band can be effectively employed to make the key function properly. Be careful not to bind or hinder the action of an adjacent key.

Loose Bridge Adjusting Screws

Set the adjusting screw for the proper bridge action and place a drop of clear fingernail polish on the screwhead.

Loose Thumb Rest

Use transparent tape to hold it on the body.

Loose Key Guard (bassoon and saxophone)

Using a piece of French horn valve cord, tie the guard flange down against the body.

Bridge Key Not Closing

Place a small piece of tape or paper with glue under the bridge arm to make the pads close in unison.

Unsoldered Tone Holes (saxophone)

Seal the leaks with clear fingernail polish.

BRASSES

Leaking Water Keys

Loop a rubber band around the water key just above the cork.
    For missing corks, use a piece of adhesive tape across the nipple.

Unsoldered Braces

Wrap several strands of French horn valve cord around the solder flange and tighten it snugly against the tubing.

Unsoldered Finger Hooks

Use French horn valve cord and transparent tape to attach the finger hook in position.

Leaking Tubing

Acid holes and cracks can be sealed, temporarily, by transparent tape, contact cement, or clear fingernail polish.

Leaking Soldered Joints

1. Clean the area.
2. Apply contact cement or clear fingernail polish to the leak.

Extremely Loose Second Valve Slides
(cornet and trumpet)

Loop a rubber band around the pull knob and the valve casing, or seal each joint with transparent tape.

Repairing Valve Springs

Stretch the springs if they are weak. Cut off one or two loops if they are too strong, and bend the severed end coils until the spring will stand erect when placed on that end.

Broken French Horn Lever Spring

Loop a heavy rubber band, or several small ones, over the valve cap and under the lever.

Missing String Screw on French Horn Key

Pass the string through the threaded hole on the lever arm and tie it securely.
    If the missing screw is on the stop arm, use the string screw from the lever arm on the stop arm, and tie the string to the lever arm.

Missing Water Key Screw, Hinge Rod,
or Pivot Screw

Use a round toothpick, or a wooden match tapered to a point, for an axle or pivot point.

Broken Braces on Fiberglass Sousaphones

Using a small block of Styrofoam as a spacer between the brass and fiberglass tubings, wrap several strands of tape around both tubings to secure the Styrofoam and to effect rigidity.

SNARE DRUM

Broken Heads

Keeping spare heads on hand is the only sure solution.

Small Dents in Plastic Timpani Heads

Some timpanists hold a lit cigarette closely to the dent while moving it in a brushing motion. The heat is said to eliminate the dent.

INSTRUMENT CASE

Broken Handle

Make a handle with a coat hanger, pad it with rags or paper, and wrap it with friction or plastic tape.

Broken Latches or Hinges

Loop a belt or rope around the case.

Locked Case, Lost Key

Place a screwdriver under the latch and rap the case lock smartly with a rawhide mallet.

A collection of assorted case keys kept in the repair kit will eliminate this problem.

Loose Case Lining

Reglue the lining, using contact cement.

Selected Projects 7

The projects begin with the easy operations and progress to the difficult ones in each section. To prevent costly mistakes, assignments (or attempts) should be made in sequence, beginning with the brass instruments.

PISTON INSTRUMENTS

Project 1

    A. Clean a brass mouthpiece

    B. Install a water key cork

    C. Loosen a stuck valve cap

    D. Pull a stuck mouthpiece

    E. Install a water key spring

Project 2

    A. Loosen stuck tuning bits (sousaphone)

    B. Straighten a bent shank on a mouthpiece

    C. Pull a stuck slide (first, second, or third)

    D. Pull a stuck, main tuning slide

Project 3

    A. "Free up" a sluggish valve

    B. Realign the piston ports

Project 4

Locate and remove an obstruction from the tubing

Project 5

Internal clean a cornet or trumpet

Project 6

Internal clean a baritone

Project 7

Remove the brass valve section from a fiberglass sousaphone and internal clean the entire instrument

Project 8

Remove dents from the bell taper of a cornet or trumpet

Project 9

Remove dents from a valve casing (cornet or trumpet)

ROTARY VALVE INSTRUMENTS

Project 1

    A. Level the levers

    B. Restring the valves

    C. Align the rotors

    D. Install new bumper corks

Project 2

Remove all slides, clean the slides and the slide sleeves, grease them, and replace them

Project 3

Remove one rotor, clean it, oil it, and replace it

Project 4

Internal clean a French horn

TROMBONES

Project 1

    A. Install a new water key cork

    B. Install a new water key spring

    C. Unstick a frozen bell taper

    D. Remove dents in the bell taper

Project 2

    A. Pull a stuck tuning slide

    B. Install new slide bumpers

Project 3

Internal clean a trombone

Project 4

"Free up" a hand slide

FLUTE

Project 1

A. Swab all joints

B. Vacuum test all joints

C. Adjust a bridge screw

D. Recork a key

E. Clean and oil the upper C or the G hinge rod and tube

F. Reset a tuning cork

Project 2

A. Install a pad in upper C

B. Install a pad in A or B♭

C. Adjust the bridge from low C to C♯

D. Remove loose action in any of the keys

Project 3

Dismantle all keys, clean the keys and body parts, oil the screws, reassemble the instrument, and check it; recork, adjust the bridges, and reseat the pads as needed

Project 4

Install a new tuning cork

Project 5

    A. Expand a head joint tenon

    B. Expand a foot joint tenon

Project 6

    A. Install a flat spring

    B. Install a needle spring

Project 7

    A. Remove dents from a head joint

    B. Remove dents from a foot joint

Project 8

Completely repad a flute (include cleaning, recorking and straightening the keys where needed, retensioning the springs, oiling them, and adjusting them)

SOPRANO CLARINET

Project 1

    A. Clean a mouthpiece

    B. Swab all joints

    C. Vacuum test the upper and lower joints

    D. Oil the bore of a wooden clarinet

    E. Clean and oil a rusted pivot screw

Project 2

    A. Clean and oil a hinge rod and tubing

    B. Recork a key

   C. Regulate the adjusting screw from A$^\flat$ to A

   D. Adjust the forked E$^\flat$-B$^\flat$ bridge

   E. Adjust the low E-F bridge

Project 3

   A. Install silencer skins in the levers

   B. Install a large pad (lower joint)

   C. Recork a thumb rest

Project 4

   A. Recork a tenon

   B. Replace a flat spring

   C. Replace a needle spring

Project 5

   A. Remove tone hole chips

   B. Reset a loose post

Project 6

   A. Eliminate sluggish key action

   B. Straighten a key

   C. Tighten a tenon ring

Project 7

   A. Patch a broken tone hole on a ring key

   B. Adjust a ring key for proper level

Project 8

Repair a stripped thread

Project 9

Reset a tapered tube on a register key

Project 10

    A. Remove loose action from a key with a tapered pivot screw (post reamer)

    B. Relieve pressure from a tapered pivot screw (pivot screw reamer)

Project 11

Remove fuzzy sound from any note except low G

Project 12

    A. Remove a frozen screw

    B. Remove an object from a "stopped up" clarinet

Project 13

Remove all keys and levers, clean the body, keys, and levers; replace the pads and corks where needed; oil all screws; reassemble, adjust, and test the instrument

Project 14

Completely repad a clarinet

ALTO AND BASS CLARINETS

Project 1

    A. Adjust the octave key mechanism

    B. Adjust the bell E♭ key for closure with E and F

Project 2

Adjust the bridge keys on the upper and lower stacks

Project 3

With a leak light and/or feeler, check all pads for seating and all bridge mechanisms for proper closures of companion pads

Project 4

Disassemble all keys and levers, clean the body, keys, levers, hinge rods, and tubes; recork and install new pads where needed; oil all screws, reassemble the instrument, and test it

NOTE: On an alto or bass clarinet that has a tension band holding the upper and lower joints together, loosen the band screw and separate the two joints before disassembling the instrument.

OBOE

Project 1

    A. Vacuum test the upper and lower joints for leaks

    B. Adjust for proper clearance between bridges from the F♯ key to the side B♭ and C teeter

    C. Adjust the bridge between F♯ and G♯

    D. Check the bridges for D trill

E. Check the octave mechanisms for proper closure of each key

Project 2

A. Adjust the bridges for equal pressure between companion pads in the lower stack

B. Adjust the low B and B$\flat$ for unison closings

Project 3

Install and seat a pad in any of the following: low B$\flat$, B, C, C$\sharp$, or E$\flat$

Project 4

Disassemble the upper joint, clean the body, keys, levers, hinge rods, and hinge tubes; recork and replace pads where needed; adjust or replace any of the flat and needle springs if needed; oil all screws, reassemble the instrument, and check it.

Project 5

Disassemble the lower joint and follow the procedures in Project 4 above

BASSOON

Project 1

Insert the tenor joint into the boot joint and the bocal into its socket, and adjust the piano or whisper key for proper bridge action and closure

Project 2

Use a leak light (or a feeler if the pads are not kidskin) and check all pads in the bass and bell joints

Project 3

Adjust the low B♭ , B, C, and D for unison closings

Project 4

Using a leak light with a small bulb and/or a feeler, check all pads on the tenor joint

Project 5

Using both leak light bulbs and a feeler, check the pad seatings and bridge operations in the boot joint

Project 6

Vacuum test all joints

Project 7

Using an assistant, place the boot joint into a shallow container of water so that the water level comes just above the end bow flange; stop one socket of the boot joint and blow into the other socket to determine if a leak is present around the body flange or the cork flange

Project 8

Recork an end bow

Project 9

Disassemble a tenor joint, clean all parts, oil the screws, and reassemble it

Project 10

Disassemble a bass joint, clean all parts, oil the screws, and reassemble it

NOTE: Except for minor repairs (key corking, installing macaroni, installing or reseating easy pads, etc.), attempts to disassemble the boot joint, to completely repad a bassoon, or to attempt other repairs not given should be avoided by the novice.

SAXOPHONE

Project 1

    A. Recork a key

    B. Install macaroni on a key

    C. Refelt a key guard (bumper)

    D. Install a felt disc

    E. "Free up" a sticking $G\sharp$ pad

Project 2

    A. Install and seat a pad in a palm key

    B. Install and seat a pad in a low $D\sharp$ key

    C. Reseat a pad in the lower stack

Project 3

    A. Remove, clean, and oil a key roller

    B. Install a flat spring

    C. Install a needle spring

Project 4

Install a neck cork

Project 5

"Free up" a sluggish key that has been caused by a bent post

Project 6

Straighten an octave teeter and adjust the octave mechanism for correct action

Project 7

Adjust the upper stack bridge keys (A, B♭, B, and C) for unison closings

Project 8

Adjust the lower stack bridge keys

Project 9

    A. Expand a neck tenon

    B. Level a tone hole

Project 10

    A. Adjust the low B to B♭ bridge

    B. Adjust the bridge from F♯ to B♭ and G♯

Project 11

Disassemble all keys, levers, and teeters, clean all parts, pad and cork where needed, oil the parts, and reassemble them

Project 12

Completely repad a saxophone

Terminology[*] 8

Since a *complete* list of terms used in the repair industry would be of no practical value to the band director, and since repair jargon varies geographically, the following list contains (with a few exceptions) only the generally accepted terms with which the average director or instrumentalist will come in contact. While many terms will seem elementary or unnecessary to some readers, they will prove beneficial to others.

No attempt has been made to give prices on repair items, or to make definitive statements regarding repair practices. Price changes are frequent throughout the instrument industry, and repair philosophies vary from city to city.

ACTION ROD: A short rod, usually glass, that operates through the body of the boot joint of a bassoon to open and close pads on the opposite sides of the body.

ADJUSTING SCREW: A screw on woodwind **bridge keys** or feet for obtaining equal pressure between pads that close simultaneously; for eliminating slack; or, on some brands, for adjusting pad openings to improve intonation.

BALANCER: The weight attached to a trombone tuning slide that helps overcome the leverage produced by the hand slide.

BAND: 1. A metal ring that is compressed into a precut groove on a cracked woodwind to prevent the crack from widening.

*Terms in this chapter are set in bold type wherever they first appear in the text. **167**

2. The repair of a cracked woodwind; e.g., "to band."

BAR: A metal or wooden tone block common to all keyboard type percussion instruments.

BEARING WASHER: A thick washer with an extended hole, through which the short stem of a **rotary valve** is inserted.

BELL BOW: The final, large, curved tubing preceding the beginning flare of the bell.

BELL RING: *See* Tenon Ring.

BELL SCREW: A screw that holds the bell of a brass instrument in position.

BELL SPUD: A small, round **nut** attached to a **flange** that receives the **bell screw**.

BLOW HOLE: The opening in the **lip plate** of a flute or piccolo into which air is blown to produce sound.

BOCAL: A bassoon **neckpipe** or **crook**.

BOOSTER: A plastic or metal disc that attaches (or is attached to) a woodwind pad to boost the tone.

BORE:
1. The opening in all wind instruments through which the sound waves pass.
2. The size of such openings.

BOTTOM CAP: *See* End Bow.

BOW: The curved tubing on brass and woodwind instruments.

BOW CAP: The protector cap that fits over the **end bow** on a bassoon butt joint.

BOW KNOB: The knob that is soldered to the small bow on brass instrument slides to facilitate removal of the slides.

BRACE: A round, square, or hexagonal rod, usually brass, that is attached to **flanges** or **sockets** to maintain stability between instrument parts.

BRACKET: A catchall term used to describe a brace, extension, socket, guard, arm, etc.

BRIDGE: *See* Yoke.

BRIDGE KEY: A woodwind key containing a special arm that actuates another arm for opening and closing **key cups** simultaneously.

BRIGHT DIP: *See* Dip.

BUMPER: The felt, cork, plastic, or rubber attached to keys, **levers**, **braces**, slides, **cork barrels**, or finger buttons to prevent a metallic "click" when actuating the moving parts.

BURNING IN: Heating the **pad cups** on a woodwind key while depressing the key in order to **seat** the pad correctly on the **tone hole**.

BURNISH: The use of a smooth, file-shaped tool to "rub out" dents on brass instruments—especially on the bell part—and to polish plated instruments where buffing is impractical.

BUTT:
1. The boot joint of a bassoon.
2. The large bow on a saxophone.
3. *See* **Snare Butt**.

CASING: The walls (or housing) of a **piston** or **rotary valve**.

CHAMBER:
1. The resonating section of a woodwind mouthpiece.
2. Sometimes used synonymously with **bore**.

COLOR BUFF (or COLORING): After overhaul, the final buffing with jeweler's rouge of a brass instrument that produces a "mirror" finish.

CORK BARRELS: The large **sleeves** on the upper ends of the inside slides of trombones that contain corks or springs against which the **hand slide** bumps.

COVER: Used to denote how the pads on a woodwind instrument **seat** on the tone holes. If pads are said to "cover" well, they fit evenly and allow no leaks.

CRACK WIRE: *See* Pin.

CROOK:
1. Usually, the **mouthpipe** of a bassoon.
2. Occasionally used synonymously with **slide bow**.

CROW FOOT: Same as Presser Foot.

CROWN: The cap or button that is attached to the **tuning cork** of a flute or piccolo **head joint**.

DEGREASER: A solution that removes buffing compounds from the instrument prior to **lacquering**.

DIE: A tool for making threads on the outside of a rod.

DING UP: A colloquialism meaning to do only the needed repairs to make an instrument play. Often used synonymously with **playing condition**.

DIP: A solution that cuts grime and tarnish from the interior tubings of brass instruments, leaving them with a "new" finish. Most dips can be used without harming the lacquer finish. Some repairmen, when referring to dip, precede it by using the commercial brand name.

DOC'S BAG: An outmoded case, usually of leather, for cornets and trumpets.

DRAWSTRING SACK:
1. A cloth sack with a drawstring top for holding loose articles (mouthpieces, neckpipes, key oil, cork grease, etc.) in an instrument case to prevent damage to an instrument or its finish. Size of the sack is determined by the articles to be placed inside. Heavy felt or velveteen is preferable, but any cloth material will suffice.
2. Cloth or kidskin sacks for carrying brass instruments before the advent of the modern, sturdy cases.

EMORY BUFF: The process of buffing with an emory compound.

EMORY COMPOUND: A buffing compound that is coarser than **tripoli** and used in polishing badly pitted instruments.

END BOW: The metal **bow** or curved tubing with an attached **flange** that connects the two **bores** at the bottom of the **butt** joint on a bassoon.

END CAP: *See* Bow Cap (bassoons).

END CAP: *See* Tenon Cap (woodwinds).

END PLUG: A plug inserted in the small end of a saxophone (where the **mouthpipe** fits) to prevent bending the **octave bridge** when the saxophone is placed in the case.

FEELER: A small dowel (about the size of a wooden match) with a thin strip of cellophane attached to one end. It is used to locate light or heavy pressure areas on woodwind pads.

FERRULE: A short, sometimes ornate, tube that connects two longer **tubes** or **sleeves**.

FINGER BUTTON: A pearl-topped cap that is screwed into a **piston valve stem**.

FINGER HOOK: A hook for the little finger (right hand) on cornets or trumpets and for the little finger (left hand) on French horns, which assists the player in locating and keeping the proper hand placement on **finger buttons** or **levers**.

FINGER RING: A ring (sometimes adjustable) on the third valve tuning slides of cornets and trumpets, by which the player adjusts the slide for proper intonation. Also called a push rod.

FISH SKIN: The thin, translucent skin that is used to cover clarinet, oboe, flute, and piccolo pads, and oboe reeds. It is also used to insert between pivot joints in **levers**.

FLANGE: The thin, metal part (usually diamond or oval shaped) on the end of a **brace**, lyre holder, **strap ring**, **bell spud**, water key **saddle**, etc., that acts as a broad holding surface when soft-soldered to an instrument body. The end **bow** on a bassoon also contains a flange.

FLAT SPRINGS: The springs mounted on woodwind keys by a small screw(s).

FLOATING IN: A process whereby extra glue is added to the pad cup to allow easier shifting of the pad. Piccolo pads, the glued pads on flutes, and some pads on other woodwinds are "floated in."

FLUSH BAND: The metal ring that is compressed into a precut groove in wooden instruments to prevent further cracking.

FLUTE PAD WASHERS: Paper washers (or **shims**) of varying diameter and thickness that are placed in the flute pad cup to allow proper **seating** of the pad.

FOOT:
1. The part of a key that touches the body (or another key) of a woodwind instrument and is usually corked or felted.
2. The part of a **key guard** that is soldered or screwed to the woodwind body (sometimes called a **guard post**).

FOOT JOINT: The short, lower joint on a flute containing the low C, C$^\sharp$, and D$^\sharp$.

GOLDBEATER'S SKIN: *See* Fish Skin.

GOOSENECK: A term used by some manufacturers and repairmen to denote the curved tubing that extends between the **neckpipe** and main tuning slide or first valve **casing** of a sousaphone. The term is also applied, by some, to any tube with a double curve, such as the curved tubing on a trombone bell.

GROMMETS: Rubber or leather cylindrical washers mounted over a retaining screw on a glockenspiel **bar.**

GUARD POST: *See* Foot, definition 2.

HAND SLIDE: The movable, outer slides of a trombone containing the **slide bow** and water key.

HARD SOLDER: Same as Silver Solder.

HEAD JOINT: The upper joint on a flute or piccolo.

HEAD JOINT CORK: Same as **Tuning Cork.**

HINGE ROD: A long screw, varying in length, which acts as a bearing for the **hinge tube** attached to keys on woodwinds. Each end of the screw is mounted in **posts.**

HINGE TUBE: The hollow tube that forms part of a woodwind key, into which the hinge rod is inserted.

INTERNAL CLEANING: A brass instrument term used by many repair shops to denote the removal of slides, valves, and water keys, immersion in a soap solution, scrubbing tubing interiors with brushes, rinsing and regreasing slides and valve caps. Though practice varies from shop to shop, new corks and felts, valve alignment, and removal of accessible dents are often included.

JOINT CAP: Same as Tenon Cap.

JOINT COVER: Same as Tenon Cap.

JOINT LOCK: A mechanism for holding two woodwind joints (specifically bassoons) in proper position after assembling.

KEY CUP: The cup attached to woodwind keys that holds the pad.

KEY GUARD: A metal **bracket** that partially surrounds a **tone hole** to prevent damage to an exposed key. It is attached by soldering to the body or by screws to guard "feet."

KEY GUIDE: A U-shaped metal tab that guides a long woodwind key back into correct position on its **tone hole** when the key is released.

KEY ROLLER: The mother of pearl (or plastic) tubes on woodwind keys that provide a smoother, more rapid change of finger positions.

KNUCKLE: The short, curved tubing attached to the valve **casing**, onto which the tuning slide **sleeves** are soldered.

LACQUER:
1. The clear liquid that is sprayed on instruments after polishing to prevent tarnishing.
2. The process of lacquering; i.e., "to lacquer."

LAPPING: A process of polishing (or honing) brass instrument valves with pumice and oil, whereby the valve is pushed, pulled, and rotated in the valve casing, or in a "lapping block," to ensure precision fitting.

LEAK LIGHT: A device for detecting pad leaks in woodwind instruments when the keys are closed.

LEVELING WEDGE: A metal wedge used in leveling the pads on a saxophone.

LEVER:
1. A woodwind key without a **pad cup**, usually operating on a fulcrum.
2. Any arm that actuates another moving part (i.e., the valve lever on a French horn).

LIP PLATE: The attachment on a piccolo or flute head **joint** on which the lower lip is placed.

LOCK PLATE: A small plate attached to the body of some woodwind instruments that prevents the **post** from turning.

LUG:
1. An ambiguous term denoting any type of device (**nut, spud,** etc.) for fastening or spacing two parts.

2. A nickel-plated or chrome-plated **bracket** that is attached, by screws, to the side of a drum shell to receive the **tension rods.**

MACARONI: Rubber or neoprene tubing in varying diameters that slips over key or lever ends to prevent key noises.

MANDREL: A wooden or metal rod, sometimes tapered, to hold instruments in a vise while cleaning, soldering, etc.; or a rod utilized as a "backup" while removing dents by **burnishing.**

MOUTHPIECE RECEIVER: A small ornate tube (or **ferrule**) that reinforces or strengthens the **mouthpipe** where the mouthpiece is inserted.

MOUTHPIPE: The tubing into which the mouthpiece is inserted in brass instruments, or onto which the mouthpiece is placed on woodwind instruments (**neckpipe**).

MUTTON TALLOW: The rendered fat from sheep. Most meat departments will give this tallow to customers at no charge. It can be cut into small chunks and slowly melted in a skillet. When the melting action is completed, the tallow should be poured into its final container. When cooled, it forms a white substance similar to cork grease.

NECKPIPE: The curved metal **tube** on saxophones and large clarinets into, or onto, which the mouthpiece is placed. Bassoon **bocals** are also referred to as **neckpipes.**

NEEDLE SPRINGS: The needlelike springs that are mounted in woodwind **posts** (or, in rare cases, mounted on a key).

NIB: The small, **nipple**-like **tube** on a bassoon **bocal** that contains a vent hole for the **whisper key**.

NIPPLE: A small, round piece of metal (soft-soldered to tubing) on which the water key cork seats.

NUT: A round (usually knurled), square, or hexagonal piece of metal that contains a threaded hole.

OCTAVE BRIDGE: The mechanism on a saxophone (usually protruding beyond the **tenon receiver**) that actuates the upper octave key on the neckpipe.

OCTAVE TONE HOLE: *See* Octave Tube.

OCTAVE TUBE: The **tube** inserted through the body of woodwind instruments, especially at the octave or register key and the thumb, to prevent moisture from clogging the opening.

OVERHAUL: The most complete repair of an instrument. The following items are generally included:
A. Woodwinds:
    1. All keys are removed from the instrument and all needle springs are

removed from the posts.

2. Thorough cleaning of body parts, inside and out (the lacquer is removed from brass saxophones).
3. Body parts are polished (dents in metal woodwinds are removed and brass-finished saxophones are also **lacquered.**
4. All joints, **neckpipes,** or **tenons** are recorked and refitted. Some repairmen do not remove **tenon** corks if they are new or in good condition.
5. Trademarks are regilded or resilvered, or new decals are placed on some plastic instruments.
6. All keys and levers are polished (brass-finished saxophone keys are also **lacquered**). An extra charge is usually made for replating nickel or other plated keys that have become worn from use.
7. New **bumper** corks are installed on all keys.
8. Old pads are removed and replaced with new pads (the only exception being that *good* cork pads on oboes and clarinets are usually left intact, since cork does not deteriorate like skin pads).
9. Rust and gummy solutions are removed from **hinge rods** and **hinge tubings.**
10. **Hinge rods, hinge tubing,** and **pivot screws** are oiled.
11. New **silencer skins** are installed in **levers.**
12. All pads are seated for proper **coverage.**
13. Loose action is removed from worn keys.
14. All loose **posts** are tightened.
15. Loose bell and **tenon rings** are tightened.
16. Bent keys and **levers** are straightened.
17. Broken or rusted springs are replaced.
18. Bassoons: a new gasket is installed on a leaking **end bow.**
19. Flutes and piccolos: new head joint corks are installed.
20. **Tone hole** nicks and chips are removed.
21. The instrument is thoroughly checked for proper mechanical operation and intonation.
    NOTE: Again, repair shop practices vary according to the seriousness of additional repair problems and the overhaul price. But other items that should be included in an overhaul are: silver soldering broken parts, installing **tenon caps,** repairing or replacing cracked **tone holes,** shortening joints, refacing mouthpieces, etc.

B. Brasses:
1. All slides, valves, water keys, tuning mechanisms, and valve caps are removed.
2. Lacquered instruments are placed in a solution for removal of old lacquer.
3. Interior is cleaned and scrubbed thoroughly.

4. Broken, leaking, or loose parts are soldered.
5. Accessible parts of the entire instrument (including screws) are rough **buffed** with an **emory** or **tripoli** compound.
6. All dents are removed.
7. All parts of the instrument are **pickled** or **dipped**.
8. Pits in the instrument caused from body acids are removed (unless too deep) by sanding, **emory buffing, strapping**, and by a second rough **buffing** with **tripoli**.
9. Parts of the instrument not **rough buffed** are **ragged**.
10. Instrument is buffed with white rouge. (This step is omitted by some shops.)
11. Bell interior is polished as deeply as practical.
12. The instruments and parts are **color buffed** or **rouged**.
13. Instrument is placed in **degreaser**, cleaned, and dried.
14. All instrument parts are **lacquered**.
15. Instrument is then recleaned inside to remove buffing and lacquer dust.
16. Slides and **valve caps** are greased, new felts and corks installed (new strings on French horns), and valves are properly aligned and oiled. *NOTE:* The finishing treatment for plated instruments varies. Plated instruments with smooth finish are **burnished** and **color buffed**; satin-finished instruments are **burnished** and scratch brushed; neither type is **lacquered** except by special request of the customer.

C. Percussions:

Overhauling and refinishing most percussion instruments are not normal services of the average repair shop, since the cost would be as much or more than the cost of a new instrument. Frequent changes in styles, designs, and finishes also make percussion overhauls impractical. Mallet instruments (timpani, chimes, vibes) should be sent to the factory for major repairs.

PAD BOOSTER: *See* Booster.

PAD CUP: Same as Key Cup.

PAD SCREW: The metal screw that fits through the **pad washer** on flutes.

PAD SLICK: A thin, metal slat of varying shapes that is used in shifting pads for correct seating.

PAD SPUD: A small, threaded, metal **tube** or disc that is soldered into the bottom of a **pad cup** to receive the pad screw (on most flutes and some saxophones).

PAD WASHER: A small metal disc that holds the flute pad in place.

PALM KEYS: The keys on a saxophone operated by the palm of the left hand (upper D, D♯, and F).

PAPER WASHERS: Washers of varying diameters and thicknesses placed under flute pads to ensure proper **seating**.

PIANO KEY: Same as Whisper Key.

PICKLE: An acid solution in which instrument parts are immersed for cleaning.

PIN:
1. A small threaded rod that is screwed into wooden instruments to prevent cracks from widening.
2. The repair of a cracked woodwind; i.e., "to pin."

PIN VISE: A pencil-like device for holding **needle springs**.

PISTON: The valve part that operates vertically inside the valve casing.

PIVOT SCREW: The short screw mounted in **posts** on woodwind instruments on which the key turns or pivots.

PLATEAU:
1. The disc on a closed **pad cup** over a **tone hole** on which the finger is placed (alto and bass clarinets), as opposed to the open tone hole with a ring key (soprano clarinets).
2. The offset or extended disc operated by a finger that closes a pad (piccolo; first-finger "C" on a flute; first-finger (left hand) F♯ and third-finger (right hand) G-D on an alto or bass clarinet, etc.).
3. *See* **Table Key**.

PLAYING CONDITION: The third most complete repair of an instrument, following 1) **overhaul** and 2) **repad** (woodwinds) or **internal cleaning** (brasses). For woodwinds: to install new pads where needed, straighten bent keys, recork joints or keys where needed, reseat leaking pads, solder broken keys, replace broken springs, and remove key noises, etc. For brasses: to resolder loose parts, pull stuck mouthpieces, remove accessible dents, pull and grease all slides, replace bad water key corks, and "free up" valves. Some repairmen use the term interchangeably with "**ding up**" and **internal cleaning**.

PORT: An opening in a **piston** through which the tone passes.

POST: The knoblike part mounted to the body of a woodwind instrument that holds the **pivot screw, hinge rod**, or **key guard**.

POST LOCK: A device for preventing a woodwind **post** from turning. It can be one of several devices—a **set screw, lock plate**, etc.

PRESSER FOOT (frequently called "crow foot"): The part of a woodwind key against which another key or bridge presses to operate both keys simultaneously. Specifically, the forked arm on the clarinet low F.

PROTECTOR CAP: The removable cap at the base of a bassoon butt joint that protects the **end bow** from damage. Sometimes used erroneously for **Tenon Cap.**

PULL KNOB: Same as **Bow Knob.**

PULL RING: On French horns, the ring that is soldered onto the **slide bow** to permit easy removal of the tuning slide.

PUMICE: A fine abrasive powder used in **lapping, strapping**, polishing, and tightening loose posts.

PUSH ROD: *See* **Finger Ring.**

RAGGING: A process of using a rag, saturated with polish, in a "shoeshining" motion to produce a glossy finish around valve casings and tubings that cannot be reached with a buffing wheel.

RAILS: The flat edges on the sides of the open **chamber** on a single-reed mouthpiece on which the reed lays.

REAMER: A drill-like tool for enlarging holes, which leaves a smooth finish for precision fittings. Often used on out-of-round or dented valve casings prior to **lapping.**

RECEIVER: The reinforced **tube** on the end of a **mouthpipe** (brasses) into which a mouthpiece is inserted.

REGISTER TUBE: Same as **Octave Tube.**

REPAD: (Woodwinds only): The second most complete repair of a woodwind instrument. Generally, to remove all old pads and replace with new ones. Specifically:
1. Remove all keys from the instrument.
2. Clean the instrument body parts. (Plastic and metal woodwinds can be scrubbed with soap and water.)
3. Clean all keys.
4. Straighten bent **hinge rods, tubings**, and keys.
5. Clean rust and gum from *all* hinge rods and tubings, and oil.
6. Remove *all* old pads and replace with new ones, preferably double skin pads.
   Exception: cork oboe and clarinet pads in good condition should be left untouched.
7. Replace missing **bumpers.**
8. Repair chipped **tone holes**.
9. Seat all keys for proper **coverage.**
10. Install new **fish skins** in **lever** pivot points.
11. **Pickle** the mouthpiece.
12. Test for leaks and for correct key action.
    NOTE: Although an additional charge will be made by most repairmen,

bad **tenon** corks, loose **posts**, broken springs, and loose key action should be remedied while being repadded to prevent additional trips to the repair shop.

ROCKER: Same as Teeter.

ROTARY VALVE: A type of valve (such as on the French horn) with a rotating motion, as opposed to the "pumping" action of a **piston** type valve.

ROTOR: Same as **Rotary Valve.**

ROUGE:
1. A red polishing compound used in **color buffing**.
2. The process of color buffing; i.e., to "rouge" an instrument.

ROUGH BUFF: The use of **tripoli** on a buffing wheel, which removes tarnish during the first buffing process.

ROUGING: Same as Color Buffing.

SADDLE:
1. Same as **Yoke**.
2. Sometimes used in referring to the **thumb saddle**.

SCRATCH BRUSH: A process using a soap solution with a soft, brass, rotating brush for restoring the lustre to a satin-finished, plated instrument.

SEAT: A term similar to **Cover**. To "seat a pad" means to level it so that all sides touch evenly on the **tone hole** rim.

SET SCREW: A tiny screw inserted in a **post** at a ninety-degree angle to a pivot screw or brace rod to lock it in place.

SHANK: Usually, the tapered end of a brass mouthpiece that fits into the mouthpiece receiver.

SHIM: A thin, paper or metal strip that is placed between two instrument parts to remove looseness. Paper **washers** are also called shims.

SICKLE: A sickle-shaped **teeter** key that is mounted, with a screw, to the body of some models of the alto and bass clarinets. Its action effects the correct opening and closing of the two register key pads.

SILENCER SKINS: **Fish skins** that are placed on the ends of clarinet **levers** to reduce the key noise.

SILVER SOLDER: The use of a silver alloy for soldering broken keys or instrument parts where a strong connection is needed.

SLEEVE: A **tube** that slips into or over another tube, or a tube that connects two parts of an instrument, making them as one.

SLICK: *See* Pad Slick.

SLIDE BOW:
1. The short U-shaped tubing that is **soft-soldered** into the **sleeves** of a tuning slide.
2. The curved tubing at the bottom end of the trombone hand slide.

SLIDE CROOK: Same as **Slide Bow.**

SLIDE KNOB: Same as **Bow Knob.**

SMUGGLER'S CASE: A tubular, leather or oil cloth-covered, cardboard case that was once in vogue for carrying the Albert System clarinet.

SNARE BUTT: A **bracket** for holding a snare. It is mounted on the opposite side of the shell from the snare release mechanism.

SOAP BARK: A soap solution used with water when **scratch brushing.**

SOCKET: A recessed (or "drilled out") area in instruments into which a protruding part of equal size is inserted. Specifically, the recessed joint on a woodwind instrument into which the **tenon** is inserted.

SOFT SOLDER: The lead and tin alloy used in soldering broad surfaces together where stress is light.

SPACER: A **tube, shim,** or washer of varying materials, sizes, and designs used to eliminate slack between keys or any parts of an instrument.

SPATULA: The flat, or slightly arced, part of a woodwind key or **lever** that is operated by the fingers.

SPOT LACQUER: A process used in some shops whereby a small lacquered area that has been burned by soldering, or worn off by wear, is polished and re-lacquered.

SPRING BLOCK: A small, metal, grooved part of a woodwind key or body that holds the **needle** or **flat spring** in place when the key is in proper position.

SPRING CLAMP: A scissorlike clamp that holds a woodwind pad against the tone hole for creating a firm **seat** or ring on the pad.

SPRING HOOK: A device resembling a crochet needle that has a hook and groove on one end for attaching **needle springs** to the **spring block.**

SPUD:
1. The threaded **tube** on the bell receiver ring of sousaphones, baritones and alto horns.
2. A recessed snap receiver on some brands of bassoons.
3. *See* **Pad Spud.**

STACK: A group of keys operated by one hand—such as the G, A, B♭ , and C keys (upper stack) operated by the left hand on saxophones—usually connected by one long **hinge rod.**

STEM: The rod, or rodlike projection, on **pistons** and **rotary valves**.

STOCKINGS: The "swelled" portion at the bottom of the inner slide tubings on trombones that forms the main bearing surface for the **hand slide**.

STOP ARM: A brass or nickel-plated (sometimes plastic) device that is attached by a screw to a **rotary valve stem** that bumps against cork or rubber for correct alignment of the **rotor** (Figures 80 and 81, pages 112 and 113).

STOP PLATE: The flat plate attached to **rotary valve casings**. This plate holds the cork **bumpers**.

STRAPPING: Using a coarse, abrasive polish in a **ragging** motion to eliminate file marks, scratches, and pits from brass instruments.

STRAP RING: The ring on an instrument to which a back strap, neck strap, or seat strap is attached for holding the instrument while playing.

STRIP: To remove old lacquer from an instrument. Other terms associated with strip are "hot," "cold," "lye," "tank," etc.

SWEDGE: The term used by repairmen to denote the stretching, lengthening, or tightening of keys, hinge rods, hinge tubings, and **tenon rings** to prevent loose action (keys) or cracked tenon **sockets**.

TABLE KEY: A woodwind key with a broad, flat surface for operating the key (low C, D♯, C♯, B, B♭, and G♯ lever on saxophones).

TAP: A screwlike tool for making threads inside a hole.

TEETER: A seesaw or teeter-totter key that is operated by the first finger (left hand) when using the alternate, high F fingering on saxophones. Also, any key that operates in a teeter-totter motion.

TENON: The protruding end of an instrument section that fits into a **socket** or tenon **receiver**.

TENON CAP:
1. The cap placed on woodwind **tenons** to protect them from chipping and collecting dirt while in the case.
2. A metal cap that is permanently fitted to the worn or chipped tenon.

TENON RECEIVER: Same as **Socket**.

TENON RING: A metal ring that is **swedged** or soldered around the tenon **socket** on woodwinds to give added strength to the socket wall.

TENSION RODS: The threaded rods on percussions that are utilized for tightening drumheads.

THROAT: The smallest diameter of a brass mouthpiece that regulates the air flow.

THUMB HOOK: A hook, normally soldered on the body of a saxophone or French horn, which enables the player to keep a steady hand position on the keys or levers.

THUMB REST: A metal angle attached to clarinet and oboe bodies that gives the player a means of supporting the weight of the instruments and of keeping proper right-hand placement.

THUMB RING:
1. The ring on altos, baritones, tubas, and sousaphones that assists the player in maintaining proper right-hand placement.
2. A ring attached to the first valve tuning slide on some cornets and trumpets that enables the player to move the slide for proper intonation.

THUMB SADDLE: Same purpose as a **Thumb Ring** (definition 2), except that it is in a U or saddle shape.

TONE BOOSTER: *See* Booster.

TONE HOLE: The hole in woodwind instruments that is covered by the fingers or pads.

TRIPOLI: A polishing compound used for **rough buffing**.

TUBE: Any hollow, round cylinder or **sleeve** used in brass instrument construction. Also used for **tone holes** (thumb and octave) on woodwinds.

TUNING BIT: A tapered **sleeve,** fitting into the mouthpiece **receiver,** which lengthens the **mouthpipe** for proper pitch on brass instruments.

TUNING CORK: The cork in the **head joint** of a flute or piccolo that determines its tuning pitch.

TUNING OIL: A thick oil used in lining tone holes on a wooden instrument to lower the pitch.

TUNING ROD: A metal or plastic rod used in setting the **tuning cork** in the proper position in a flute or piccolo **head joint.** It also serves as a cleaning rod.

TURNBUTTON: Usually a movable, velvet-covered slat fastened by a screw. This slat holds the instrument or its parts in place inside the case.

VALVE CAP: The washerlike cap that screws into, or over, a **piston** or **rotary valve** casing. The term "valve cap" is often confused erroneously with a **finger button.**

VALVE GUIDE: The small metal or plastic tab attached to the side of a **piston,** or one of several washerlike devices with a protruding tab that operates inside the groove in a valve casing, thereby keeping the valve ports in proper alignment.

VALVE STEM: A short rod screwed into the **piston**, and into which the **finger button** is screwed.

WATER KEY: A corked, spring-mounted key for disposing of accumulated breath moisture on most brass instruments and on some large woodwind instruments. A water key is frequently referred to as a spit valve.

WHISPER KEY: The small key on a bassoon that **seats** on the **nib**.

YOKE: A U-shaped metal piece that, with the help of a screw or an axle, forms the stationary pivot point of a water key or valve trigger, etc.

Bibliography

REPAIR MANUALS

Brand, Erick D. *Band Instrument Repairing Manual.* Elkhart, Indiana: Erick D. Brand, 1946.

Nilles, Raymond J. *Basic Repair Handbook for Musical Instruments.* Fullerton, California: F. E. Olds & Son, 1959.

Tiede, Clayton H. *The Practical Band Instrument Repair Manual.* Second edition. Dubuque, Iowa: Wm. C. Brown Company Publishers, 1970.

CARE AND MAINTENANCE PAMPHLETS

Conn Corporation. *How to Care for Your Instrument.* Elkhart, Indiana [now Abilene, Texas]: C. G. Conn. Ltd., 1942.

Hovey, Nilo W. *Selmer Band Manual.* Elkhart, Indiana: H. & A. Selmer, Inc., 1955.

King Musical Instruments. *How to Care for Your Instrument. Instruction Guide for Brass Instruments.* Eastlake, Ohio: King Musical Instruments, Division of the Seeburg Corporation (N.D.).

_____. *How to Care for Your Instrument. Instruction Guide for Trombones.* Eastlake, Ohio: King Musical Instruments, Division of the Seeburg Corporation (N.D.).

_____. *How to Care for Your Instrument. Instruction Guide for Woodwinds.* Eastlake, Ohio: King Musical Instruments, Division of the Seeburg Corporation (N.D.).

Lehman, Paul R. *Teacher's Guide to the Oboe.* Elkhart, Indiana: H. & A. Selmer, Inc., 1965.

Pascucci, Vito. *Care and Minor Repairs of the Clarinet for Band Directors.* Kenosha, Wisconsin: G. Leblanc Corporation, 1959.

Pence, Homer. *Teacher's Guide to the Bassoon.* Elkhart, Indiana: H. & A. Selmer, Inc., 1963.

Weisshaar, Otto H. *Preventive Maintenance of Musical Instruments.* Melville, New York: Belwin-Mills, Inc., 1966.

REPAIR SECTIONS IN TEXTBOOKS

Richtmeyer, Lorin. "The Care and Repair of Instruments," *Music Education for Teen-agers.* Second edition. William Raymond Sur and Charles Francis Schuller. New York: Harper & Row, Publishers, 1966.

Rogers, Charles C. "Instrument Repair and Maintenance," *The Band Director's Guide.* Written and edited by Kenneth L. Neidig. Englewood Cliffs, New Jersey: Prentice-Hall, Inc., 1964.

Spohn, Charles L., and Tatgenhorst, John J. "The Care and Maintenance of Percussion Instruments," *The Percussion: Performance and Instructional Techniques,* 2nd ed. Boston: Allyn and Bacon, Inc., 1971.

Timm, Everett L. "Keeping the Key Mechanism Operative" (see also "Care" for each instrument), *The Woodwinds: Performance and Instructional Techniques,* 2nd ed. Boston: Allyn and Bacon, Inc., 1971.

Winter, James H. "Care and Maintenance" and "Slide Care," *The Brass Instruments: Performance and Instructional Techniques,* 2nd ed. Boston: Allyn and Bacon, Inc., 1969.

ANTHOLOGIES

Instrumentalist Company, The. *Brass Anthology*. Evanston, Illinois: 1974.

_____. *Woodwind Anthology*. Evanston, Illinois: 1972.
    These anthologies contain many worthwhile articles on care, maintenance, and repair.

ARTICLES IN PERIODICALS

Barzenick, W. "Hints on Clarinet Mouthpieces, Reeds, and Maintenance,"
    The Instrumentalist 26 (September 1971): 37-39.

Knaack, D. F. "Care and Repair of Percussion Instruments," *The Instrumentalist*
    25 (October 1970): 50-53.

Kuehn, D. L. "Care and Maintenance of the Tuba," *The School Musician, Director
    and Teacher* 40 (April 1969): 72-73.

Schmidt, Harry (Editor). "Clarinet Clinical: Care and Repair," *The School
    Musician, Director and Teacher* 39 (January 1967).

Sheppard, L. "The Oboe; A Plea for a Standard System of Keywork," *Music
    Teacher and Piano Student* 48 (March 1969).

Strucel, George. "Maintenance of the Horn," *The Horn Call* II, no. 1 (November
    1971): 49-53.

Thompson, W. L. "Instrument Inspections—Time Wisely Spent," *The Instrumen-
    talist* 22 (October 1968).

Windsor, R. L. "The Ten Commandments of Woodwind Upkeep," *Woodwind
    World* 10 (1971).

REPAIR SUPPLY CATALOGS

Ed Myers Company, 3022 Pacific Street, Omaha, Nebraska 68105

Erick Brand, Elkhart, Indiana 46514

Ferree's Band Instrument Tools and Supplies, 110 Calhoun Street, P.O. Box 259,
    Battle Creek, Michigan 49016.

Appendix

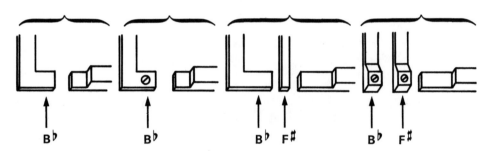

B♭   B♭   B♭   F♯   B♭   F♯

Figure 106. *Types of bridges to B♭ (Flute)*

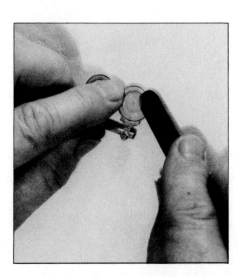

Figure 107.
Removing the tone booster (Flute)

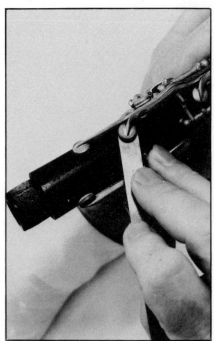

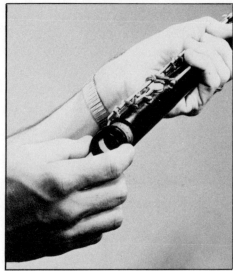

Figure 109. *The tenon cap*

Figure 108. *Using the small pad slick*

Figure 110. *Inserting a tight neckpipe*

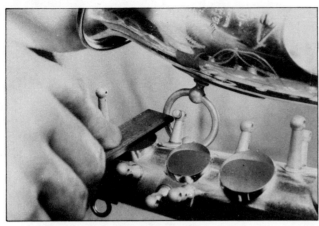

Figure 111.
*Filing the tone hole
in a close area*

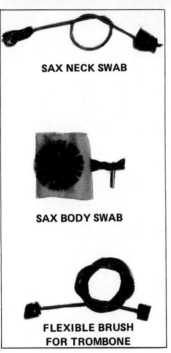

SAX NECK SWAB

SAX BODY SWAB

FLEXIBLE BRUSH
FOR TROMBONE

Figure 112. *Special swabs*

Figure 113.
*Using the key bending
tool and leveling wedge*

190

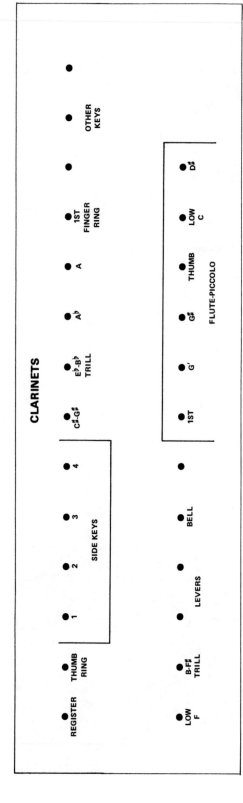

Figure 114. *The screw mounting board (Piccolo-Flute-Clarinet)*

Specifications

3/4-inch board, preferably covered with a micalike lamination

Board size: 3 1/2 inches by 12 inches
Hole size: .096 (No. 41, or 3/32 drill)
Hole depth: 3/8 inch
Screw holder: soft drink cap

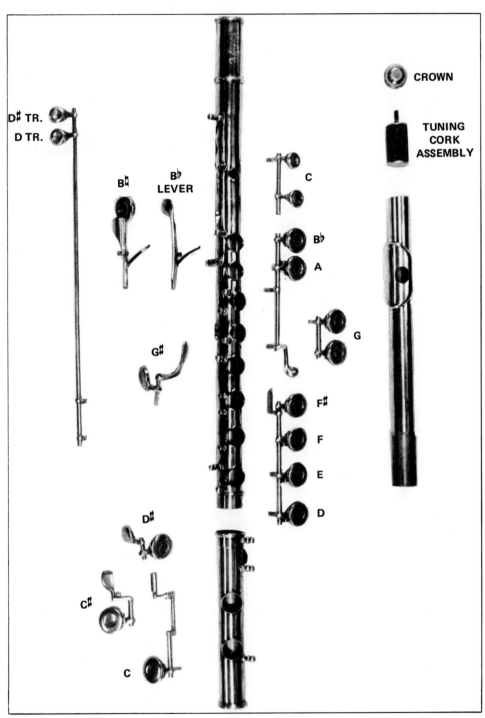

Figure 115. *The disassembled flute*

192

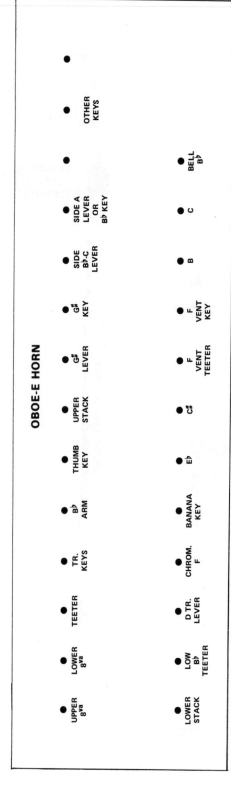

OBOE-E HORN

UPPER 8va · LOWER 8va · TEETER · TR. KEYS · THUMB KEY · Bb ARM · UPPER STACK · G# LEVER · G# KEY · SIDE Bb-C LEVER · SIDE A LEVER OR Bb KEY · OTHER KEYS

LOWER STACK · LOW Bb TEETER · D TR. LEVER · CHROM. F · BANANA KEY · Eb · C# · F VENT TEETER · F VENT KEY · B · C · BELL Bb

Figure 116. *The screw mounting board (Oboe-English horn)*

Dimensions

Board size: 3/4 inch thick by 3 1/2 inches by 12 inches
Hole size: .096 (No. 41 or 3/32 drill)
Hole depth: 5/16 inch
Screw holder: soft drink cap

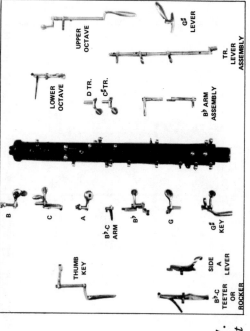

Figure 117.
The disassembled oboe, upper joint

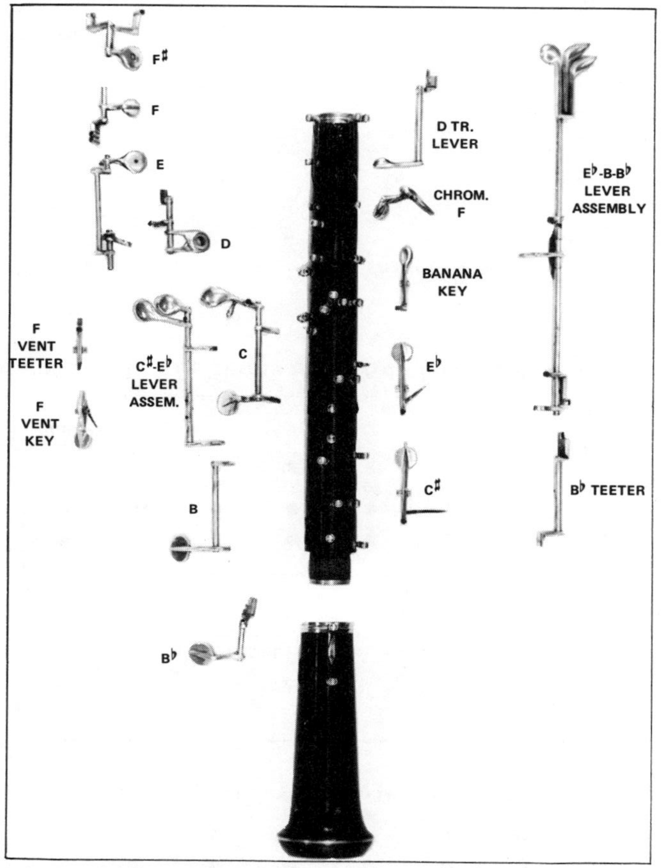

193

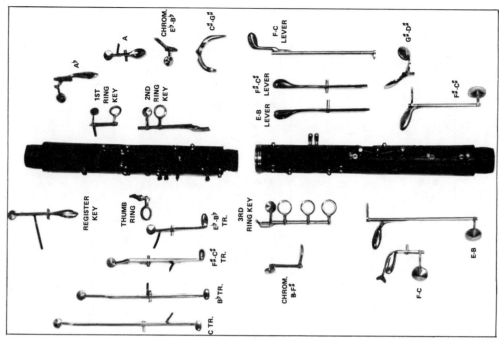

Figure 119.

The disassembled clarinet

Figure 118. *The disassembled oboe, lower joint*

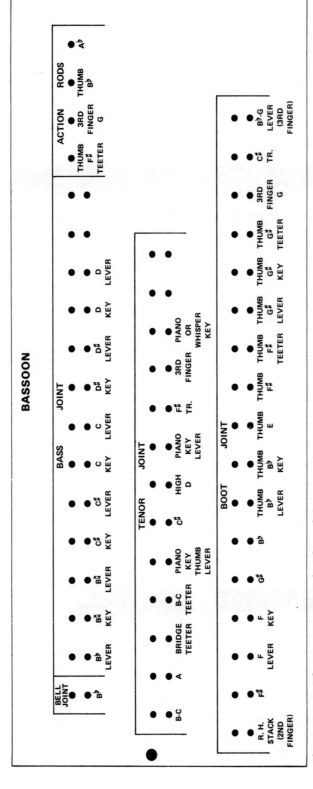

Figure 120. *The screw mounting board (Bassoon)*

Dimensions

Board size: 3/4 inch thick by 6 inches by 15 inches

Hole size: .110 (No. 35 or 7/64 drill)
Hole depth: 3/8 inch
Screw holder: Lid from a small jar

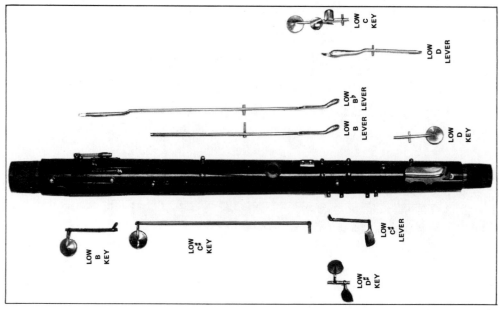

Figure 122. *The disassembled bass joint (Bassoon)*

LOW C KEY

LOW D LEVER

LOW B♭ LEVER

LOW B LEVER

LOW D KEY

LOW B KEY

LOW C♯ KEY

LOW C♯ LEVER

LOW D♯ KEY

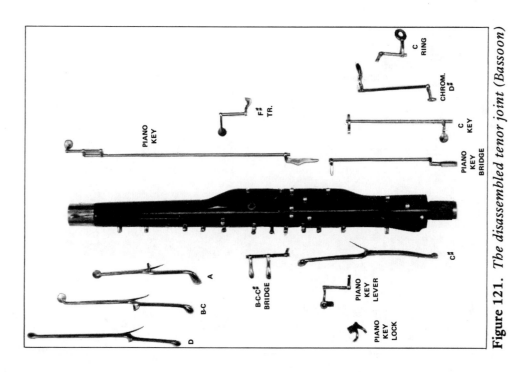

Figure 121. *The disassembled tenor joint (Bassoon)*

PIANO KEY

F♯ TR.

C RING

CHROM. D♯

C KEY

PIANO KEY BRIDGE

A

B-C

D

B-C-C♯ BRIDGE

PIANO KEY LEVER

PIANO KEY LOCK

c♯

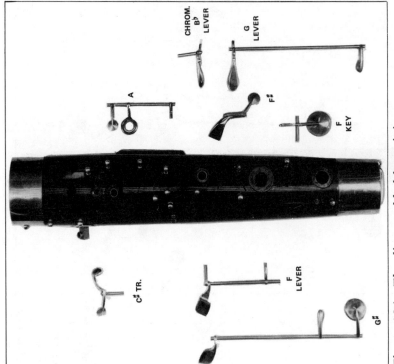

Figure 124. *The disassembled boot joint, front side (Bassoon)*

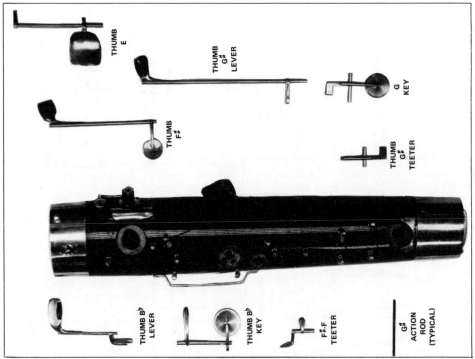

Figure 123. *The disassembled boot joint, back side (Bassoon)*

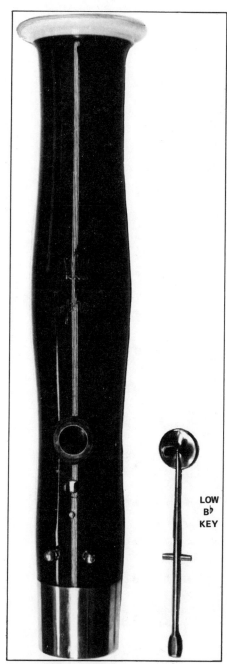

LOW
B♭
KEY

Figure 125.
The disassembled bell
(Bassoon)

198

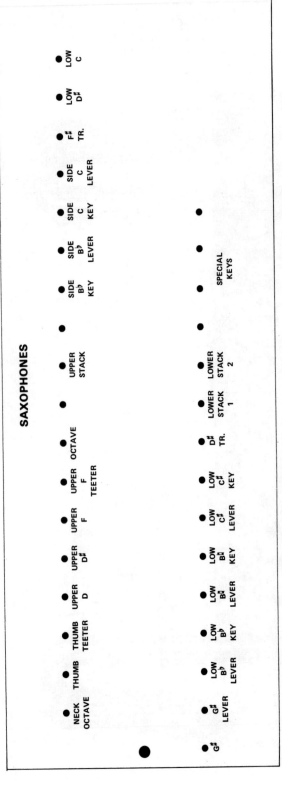

SAXOPHONES

NECK OCTAVE · THUMB LEVER · THUMB TEETER · UPPER D · UPPER D♯ · UPPER F · UPPER F TEETER · OCTAVE · UPPER STACK · SIDE B♭ KEY · SIDE B♭ LEVER · SIDE C KEY · SIDE C LEVER · F♯ TR. · LOW D♯ · LOW C

G♯ · G♯ LEVER · LOW B♭ LEVER · LOW B♭ KEY · LOW B♮ LEVER · LOW B♮ KEY · LOW C♯ LEVER · LOW C♯ KEY · D♯ TR. · LOWER STACK 1 · LOWER STACK 2 · SPECIAL KEYS

Figure 126. *The screw mounting board (Saxophone)*

Dimensions

Board size: 3/4 inch thick by 4 inches
                by 14 inches
Hole size: .116 (no. 32 or 1/8 drill)
Hole depth: 1/2 inch
Screw holder: Lid from a small jar

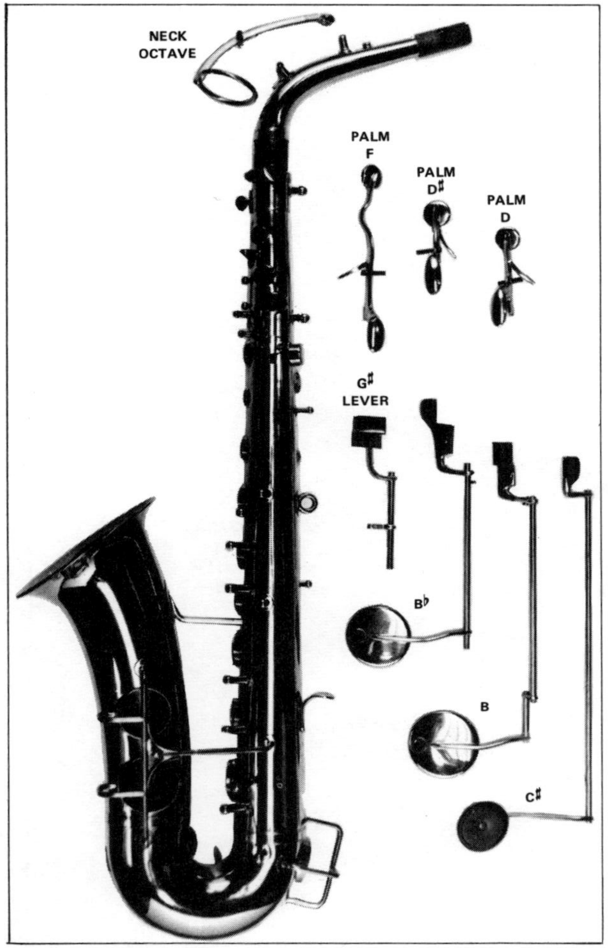

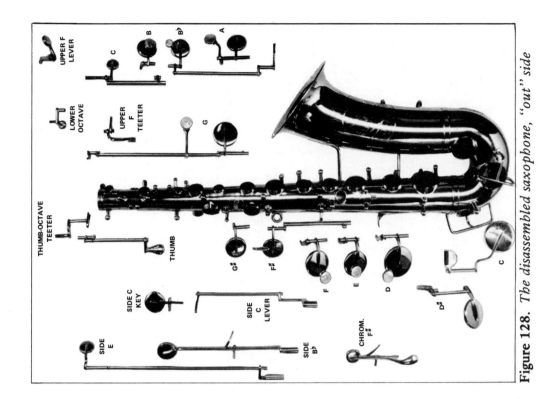

Figure 128. *The disassembled saxophone, "out" side*

Figure 127. *The disassembled saxophone, hip side*

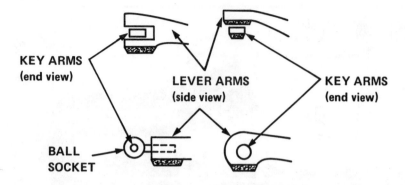

Figure 129. *Types of side key bridges (Saxophone)*

Figure 130. *The tapered mandrel (Trumpet)*

Index

D

Dents:
  bell tubing, 109
  flute, 81
  mouthpiece (brass), 37, 102–103, 146
  piston casings, 5, 106–108, 146
  saxophone body, 97
  timpani heads, 153
  tone holes, 5, 66–67, 97
  trombone slides, 115
Deposits:
  mouthpiece (brass), 37
  mouthpiece (woodwind), 9, 32, 76–77
  tone hole, 8
  trombone stockings, 118–119
Disassembling the keys:
  clarinets (alto, bass), 89
  clarinets (soprano), 84
  flute, 60
  oboe, 82–83
  saxophones, 94–95
Drying:
  brasses, 13
  woodwinds, 6, 10, 87

E

Emergency repairs (all), 149–153
End bow (bassoons):
  inspecting, 34–35
  recorking, 90–91
End plugs:
  importance, 9–10

F

Felt:
  large clarinets, 90
  saxophone keys, 93–94

P